The Homemade PIZZA COOKBOOK BIBLE

1000 Days of Authentic Recipes to Make at Home from Neapolitan, New York Style, Cheesy, Deep Dish | Including How to Make Perfect Pizza Dough at Home

Mike Gandolfini

© **Copyright 2022 - All rights reserved.**

The content contained within this book may not be reproduced, duplicated, or transmitted without direct written permission from the author or the publisher.

Under no circumstances will any blame or legal responsibility be held against the publisher, or author, for any damages, reparation, or monetary loss due to the information contained within this book. Either directly or indirectly.

Legal Notice:

This book is copyright protected. This book is only for personal use. You cannot amend, distribute, sell, use, quote, or paraphrase any part, or the content within this book, without the consent of the author or publisher.

Disclaimer Notice:

By reading this document, the reader agrees that under no circumstances is the author responsible for any losses, direct or indirect, which are incurred as a result of the use of the information contained within this document, including, but not limited to, - errors, omissions, or inaccuracies.

The information contained in this book and its contents is not designed to replace or take the place of any form of medical or professional advice; and is not meant to replace the need for independent medical, financial, legal or other professional advice or services, as may be required. The content and information in this book have been provided for educational and entertainment purposes only.

TABLE OF CONTENTS

INTRODUCTION 1

CHAPTER 1: PIZZA STYLES 3
    WHAT MAKES A PIZZA A PIZZA? 3
    THE INGREDIENTS 4
    A PLAN FOR MAKING PIZZA FOR DINNER 5
    GET GRILLING 6
    FROM COUNTERTOP TO PIZZA STONE 7
    TYPES OF COOKING 8

CHAPTER 2: TIPS AND TRICKS 10

CHAPTER 3: EQUIPMENT AND TOOLS 14
    FOOD PROCESSOR 14
    KITCHENAID MIXER 14
    PIZZA PEEL 15
    PIZZA STONE OR PIZZA STEEL 15
    RIMLESS BAKING SHEET 15
    WHEEL SLICER 15
    BENCH SCRAPER 15
    PANS 15
    ELECTRONIC SCALE 15
    SERVING TRAYS OR CARDBOARD PIZZA CIRCLES 16
    ROLLING PINS 16
    FOOD PROCESSOR OR STAND MIXER 16
    DOUGH DOCKER 16

CHAPTER 4: METHODS AND PIZZA DOUGH RECIPES 18
    THE DOUGH 18
    FLOUR 20
    YEAST 20
    WATER 20
    HIGH ALTITUDE PIZZA 21
    DOUGH MADE FROM WHEAT 21
    MIXING THE DOUGH USING A FOOD PROCESSOR 22
    ROUNDING UP THE DOUGH BALL 23

ROLLING OUT THE DOUGH 24

CHAPTER 5: 105 RECIPES (ALSO INCLUDES SWEET PIZZA) 26

1. NEW YORK STYLE PIZZA 27
2. BUTTERNUT SQUASH PIZZAS WITH ROSEMARY 29
3. CAJUN SHRIMP AND SCALLOP PIZZA 30
4. CARAMEL APPLE PIZZA 31
5. CARAMELIZED ONIONS AND RICOTTA CHEESE PIZZA 33
6. CARAMELIZED ONIONS PIZZA 34
7. CAST IRON FENNEL PIZZA 35
8. CAULIFLOWER-SPINACH PIZZA 36
9. CAULIFLOWER-VEGAN BACON PIZZA CASSEROLE 37
10. CHAFFLE PIZZA 38
11. CHEESE AND ALMOND PIZZA 39
12. CHEESE CRUST PIZZA 40
13. CHEESEBURGER PIZZA 41
14. CHEESESTEAK PIZZA 42
15. CHEESY GARLIC PIZZA 43
16. SATAY PIZZA WITH CHICKEN 44
17. DEEP DISH MEXICAN PIZZA RECIPE 45
18. MAYONNAISE BURRITO PIZZAS RECIPE 46
19. MEXICAN DEEP-DISH PAN PIZZA RECIPE 47
20. BBQ CHICKEN PIZZAS 48
21. BLT PIZZA 49
22. BACON CHEESEBURGER PIZZA 50
23. BACON AND SPINACH PIZZA 51
24. COLD VEGETABLE PIZZA 52
25. COLORFUL CRAB APPETIZER PIZZA 53
26. CORNBREAD PIZZA WHEELS 54
27. CRANBERRY CAMEMBERT PIZZA 55
28. DARTBOARD PIZZA 56
29. DILLY VEGGIE PIZZA 57
30. FANTASTIC ARTICHOKE PIZZA 58
31. FESTIVE VEGGIE PIZZA 59
32. MEXICAN PITA PIZZAS (MEXICO) RECIPE 60
33. FRESHLY BAKED PESTO PIZZA 61
34. CAULIFLOWER PIZZA 62
35. NEAPOLITAN PIZZA 63
36. SICILIAN PIZZA 64
37. GARLIC PIZZA WITH MOZZARELLA 66
38. FOUR-CHEESE PIZZA 67

39. DELICATE SEAFOOD PIZZA	68
40. PIZZA MARINARA	69
41. TUNA PIZZA	70
42. PIZZA DI MARE (WITH SEAFOOD)	71
43. VEGETARIAN PIZZA	72
44. BELL PEPPER PIZZA	73
45. PAN PIZZA CRUST	74
46. PIZZA CRUST WITHOUT YEAST	75
47. GOAT PIZZA	76
48. YEAST-FREE PIZZA DOUGH	77
49. CLASSIC TOMATO SAUCE	78
50. BASIL GARLIC SAUCE	79
51. PUMPKIN PIZZA SAUCE	80
52. WHITE PIZZA SAUCE	81
53. PIZZA NAPOLITANO	82
54. PIZZA REGINA	83
55. PIZZA CAPRICCIO	84
56. PEPPERONI PIZZA	85
57. BLACK OLIVES SALAMI PIZZA	86
58. YUMMY VEGGIE PIZZA	87
59. FRESH VEGETABLE PIZZA	88
60. VEGAN PIZZA	89
61. CHEESE PIZZA CALZONE	90
62. BUTTERMILK BISCUIT DOUGH	91
63. BUBBLE PIZZA WITH BEEF	92
64. VEGETABLE GARDEN ON PIZZA	93
65. ALFREDO PIZZA WITH SPINACH	94
66. BBQ RANCH CHICKEN PIZZA	95
67. BBQ BRISKET FLATBREAD PIZZAS	96
68. FETA SPINACH PIZZA	97
69. FRESH VEGGIE PIZZA	98
70. FRUITY BROWNIE PIZZA	99
71. SEAFOOD PIZZA	100
72. SEA AND MOUNTAINS PIZZA	101
73. HAM AND MUSHROOMS PIZZA	102
74. MEXICAN PIZZA RECIPE	103
75. MEXICAN SALMON PIZZA RECIPE	105
76. AMAZING WHOLE WHEAT PIZZA CRUST RECIPE	106
77. BASIC PIZZA DOUGH RECIPE	107
78. POURABLE PIZZA CRUST RECIPE	108
79. THIN CRUST PIZZA DOUGH RECIPE	109

80. WHOLE WHEAT PIZZA CRUST RECIPE ... 110
81. PIZZA DOUGH ... 111
82. PIZZA WITH EGG-CHEESE CRUST ... 112
83. PRO DOUGH ... 113
84. QUICK FRIED CRUST ... 114
85. ROMAN DOUGH ... 115
86. SIMPLY AMAZING PIZZA DOUGH ... 116
87. SKILLET PIZZA CRUST ... 117
88. SPELT PIZZA DOUGH ... 118
89. STUFFED CRUST ... 119
90. FRUIT PIZZA ... 120
91. PARSLEY PIZZA ... 121
92. CAULIFLOWER AND GREEN PEA PIZZA ... 122
93. RICOTTA CHEESE AND LEMON GRASS PIZZA ... 123
94. CHICKEN AND PINEAPPLE PIZZA ... 124
95. SALAMI PIZZA ... 125
96. PORK SAUSAGE PIZZA ... 126
97. TURKEY AND CARROT PIZZA ... 127
98. WHITE BUTTON MUSHROOM AND BLACK OLIVE PIZZA ... 128
99. FAST PIZZA WITH PEPPER, ZUCCHINI, AND RED ONION ... 129
100. PIZZA MARGHERITA ... 130
101. MIXED VEGGIE PIZZA ... 131
102. DELIGHTFUL VEGGIE PIZZA ... 132
103. BROCCOLI PIZZA ... 133
104. PIZZA ROLL ... 134
105. FRIED PIZZA WITH MORTADELLA AND FIORDILATTE ... 136
106. PEAR AND BRIE PIZZA ... 138

CHAPTER 6: FAQS ... 139

HOW TO COOK PIZZA IN THE HOME OVEN? ... 139
TEMPERATURE OF COOKING: ... 139
HOMEMADE PIZZA COOKING TIME: ... 139
ARE YOU USING THE RIGHT YEAST? ... 140
CHOOSING THE FLOUR: IS ONE WORTH THE OTHER? ... 140
SHOULD THE SALT BE ADDED? IF YES, WHEN? ... 140
DO I NEED TO ADD SUGAR? ... 140
ROLLING PIN; SHOULD I USE IT? ... 141
IS IT RIGHT TO FILL THE PIZZA WITH OTHER INGREDIENTS BEFORE YOU BAKE IT? ... 141
WHAT IS THE IDEAL TEMPERATURE? ... 141

CONCLUSION ... 143

ALPHABETICAL INGREDIENTS INDEX 145

INTRODUCTION

Italian cuisine can claim worldwide fame for the creation of pizza. Pizzas have a sauce base, cheese, and various toppings atop a round flatbread. While a pizza oven provides the best results for cooking, a regular oven will do in a pinch. There are pizzerias everywhere in the world. The cuisine has taken on elements from many different civilizations. However, pizza will always be a warm, satisfying, and tasty meal regardless of where you are or how you want to eat it.

Pizza is the most popular low-cost dish in the globe. It's a common staple in our diets. However, the story of how pizza went from a local favorite to a global phenomenon reveals a great deal about the movement's historical context, financial factors, and innovative shifts. For a long time, pizza has been a mainstay of the Western diet. Bits of flatbread, topped with savories, has served as an important and delightful feast for people who couldn't afford the plates' price or weren't in the mood to wait for their food for a long time.

You've found the ideal place if you're a pizza fan who's always wanted to learn how to make pizza at home. This comprehensive pizza cookbook covers every step of the pizza-making process, from preparing the dough to baking it, making the sauce, and choosing the right toppings.

For authentic pizza perfection, the dough must be made from scratch and rolled into a ball. Then you need to roll it out to get a very thin crust without any gaps. After that, pile on the toppings you like and cover everything with additional sauce and cheese.

It shouldn't come as a surprise that pizza is a popular comfort food in the United States since it is the most popular fast food in the globe. So, of course, it's tough to say no to the irresistible combination of meat, cheese, and vegetables over a flaky crust. But, rather than buying pizza, why not create your own and top it with all your favorite toppings? In this book, you'll find the easy recipes and straightforward instructions you need to make restaurant-quality pizza in the comfort of your own kitchen—time to level up your pizza-cooking abilities.

Pizza has advanced significantly from its humble street-side beginnings thanks to technological progress. These days, pizzas are baked in ovens that can be precisely controlled to provide identical results every time, and toppings are customized to suit each customer's preferences. As a result, pizza has evolved beyond simply being a pile of cheese and tomato sauce on top of some baked bread. Numerous pizza styles are available now, so you may select one that suits your palate.

To start making pizza, you should get the ingredients and put together the crust. In this way, you can customize your pizza to your tastes. This occurs due to the wide variety of pizza bases available. If you want your pizza to be delicious and crispy, you must know how to prepare it. If you want to make pizza at home but are concerned about its nutritional value, this book is your best bet.

The recipes in this book are meant to be used by home cooks of varying experience levels, adapted to suit the tastes of a wide variety of diners, and prepared in an atmosphere filled with joy and friendly banter. The atmosphere that prevails on pizza night is one of its best features. Both dinner and a lifetime of recollections are currently in the works.

Pizza can be enjoyed as a main course, a side dish, or even a snack for the whole family. It's a flexible meal that may be served at a variety of events and restaurants. Pizza's enduring appeal can be attributed partly to the combination of three of the most beloved food groups: sweet, rich, and fatty. However, the cookbook stays loyal to one of the pizza's key selling points—its low cost to make.

Though delicious on one alone, pizza's widespread appeal stems primarily from the fact that a group can enjoy it. For example, soup and sandwiches are two dishes that are best-consumed solo. Pizza, however, is intended to be shared among a large group. Therefore, the idea of the cookbook is to bring people closer together via shared meals. The pizza recipes in this booklet are given with the hope that they would encourage you to spend time with your loved ones via their preparation and sharing.

CHAPTER 1: PIZZA STYLES

What Makes A Pizza A Pizza?

Flavor balancing is half science and half art. The freshness of the ingredients should be preserved in a sea of complexity. One of our favorite pizzas has anchovies (salty, fishy) and capers (salty, herby) in a balanced proportion, much like the classic toppings mentioned here, where the emphasis is always on quality than quantity. If you don't, the whole pizza will be overly salty (remember that the dough is salted, too), and you'll keep thirsty long after you've finished eating.

When the disk is spotted or faintly burnt, the air is gently pushed from the center to the outer rim, creating a thicker crust. Because the trapped air bubbles cause the crust to be thicker, the bread rises and cooks rapidly, becoming fluffy, leavened, and easily digestible. It only takes 60–90 seconds for the thin pizza's center to be fully cooked in a traditional pizza oven firing at 900 °F+ or one of the current generation of home pizza ovens.

Creating a pizza is a fun and social activity. From a culinary perspective, this means actively using your hands and sense of touch to communicate with the ingredients. By contrast, when families eat together in the kitchen, they talk to each other facing each other in real time. Likewise, when kids have play dough in their hands, they put down their phones and enjoy the present.

The perfect pizza circle covered with fresh produce from the farmer's market may be their parents' goal, but children often have other ideas. Two examples are a Mickey Mouse pizza or a heart-shaped pie covered in red sauce. One of the best parts of having pizza night with the family is that everyone can have their own opinion while still getting along.

Pizza night might be seen as a weekly catch-up, a chance to crank up the songs and allow family life to take shape. Time spent with loved ones while enjoying delicious food? This is a no-brainer for parents and benefits everyone involved.

The Ingredients

YEAST

A living organism called yeast is required for the dough to come to life. This cookbook calls for active dry yeast in its recipes (not rapid rise or fresh yeast). In sealed paper envelopes, you can find active dried yeast in the baking aisle of any major grocery store. Add the recommended amount of yeast to the water, then wait five minutes. The liquid's surface should begin to froth. The yeast is dead if it doesn't blossom. Throw it away and begin again with a new packet.

FLOUR

If you stock up, pizza will never be far away. While authenticists swear by "00" imported Italian flour, all-purpose flour produces a good crust and is widely available. If you want to make a dough that is both tasty and durable, try mixing half bread-flour with half all-purpose flour.

SAUCE

Unlike traditional pasta sauces, pizza sauce is supposed to be spread rather than tossed. Tinned tomatoes, salt, oregano, onions, garlic, and a touch of sugar make the handmade type. It's the epitome of quick and easy cooking and may be customized with a few shakes of cayenne pepper, some fresh herbs, or a splash of vinegar. Depending on the brand, a jar of sauce can provide an incredible array of flavors, colors, and textures in a convenient, portable package.

CHEESE

Most people will only accept mozzarella: It's essential to the perfect pizza because of its melting, distinctive stretch, and creamy but firm texture. New Yorkers favor "mozz" made from cow's milk due to its low moisture level, while Neapolitans choose "mozzarella" made from water buffaloes' milk for its creamier texture.

A Plan for Making Pizza for Dinner

Being well-organized is the bedrock of successful homemade pizza making, whether you're cooking two pies or ten.

Some people prefer to plan and prepare everything separately, while others prefer to throw everything together right before serving. But regardless of how you want to make pizza, it's always a good idea to plan ahead. When making pizza for my family, I always leave a few of the preparation steps out so we can all work on them together. Children benefit from learning basic cooking skills like salad spinning, cheese slicing, grating, and sautéing onions, and they benefit even more from learning these skills alongside their families.

LET'S MAKE SOME BREAD

Put it in the fridge the dough and allow it to rise overnight, or use a previously frozen batch.

STOP AND TAKE STOCK

Make a pizza around any leftovers you have lying around, be it spinach, cherry tomatoes, or even roasted chicken and vegetables. Start with what you have on hand and make a shopping list of what you'll need to complete the recipe.

GET THE MEAT READY

The night before, brown the pepperoni, pancetta, bacon, or sausage you plan to use and store them in airtight containers in the fridge.

CHEESES THAT CRUMBLE AND MELT IN YOUR MOUTH

Cheeses like feta, Gorgonzola, and goat cheese should be crumbled the night before and stored in airtight containers in the fridge.

CLEANSING, CUTTING, AND/OR COOKING THE VEGETABLES

Broccoli should be broken down into florets, onions should be sliced, and broccoli rabe should be blanched before being chilled in sealed containers.

PREHEAT OVEN BEFORE SERVING PIZZA

Take the dough from the refrigerator and let it aside at room temp for around 40 minutes while the oven warms up.

CUT OR GRATE STRONGER CHEESES

Crumbled soft cheeses can be prepared the night before, but crumbled hard cheeses will dry out.

DON'T FORGET TO CLEAN THE GREENS

Lettuces, herbs, and other greens should be washed and spun dry before being used to top pizzas or salads.

CREATE A PIZZA BAR

Make sure everyone has their own space to shape their pizzas, and add toppings close to the oven. Put bowls of toppings on trays and label them with Post-Its to keep things organized by pizza style. Pizza makers can still experiment with different combinations, but the "recipe" is laid out for those who do not want to think too hard.

SET THE TABLE

Make it casual with stacks of plates, glasses, napkins, salad bowls, and beverages. It's a serve-yourself vibe that encourages everyone to mill around the kitchen or sit down and share slices.

Get Grilling

What is the best reason to grill pizza? It keeps the heat outside. The other best reason to grill pizza? The love! My long-established rule is that all summer entertaining (except for pig roasts) revolve around grilled pizza. The doughs are made in advance, allowing my husband and I to hang with our guests and then gather as a group to make our own pizza. The morning shopping trip is a fun part, too. We write a quick list and then head to the farmers' market to gather toppings, letting fresh ingredients spark our pizza inspiration. So much of our summer social life is built around grilling pizza. It's one of our favorite ways to rejoice in the numerous blessings of the most enjoyable time of year.

Plan a couple of practice sessions to understand the relationship between fire and dough. A learning curve to grilling pizza can be a rewarding part of a pizza journey. Plus, you can eat your mistakes.

Refrigerate prepared dough.

Get your charcoal or gas grill ready to go at least an hour before you want to cook your pizza. We're going for a very high but indirect temperature. Put the coals to one side and, if necessary, use a chimney starter to light more. Using a propane cooktop to grill? Only one burner should be lit; the other should be off. Keep the grill lid closed since hotter grills will reduce the likelihood of pizza dough sticking to the grate.

You should have everything you need easily accessible. Arrange a cutting board, a rolling pin, sauce, cheese, toppings, olive oil, salt, pepper, seasonings, a pastry brush, a spatula, and tongs on a table near the grill.

Stretch and form the dough, drizzle with olive oil, and set oil-side down on the grill near but not directly over the heat source.

After 3 minutes on the grill (time may vary depending on the heat source), spray the dough with oil, and flip it over. The dough should be covered in sauce, cheese, and your preferred toppings. Close the grill cover and cook the pizza for 4-6 minutes or until the cheese has melted. Move the pizza to a cutting board using a peel, let it cool for 2 minutes, and then slice it up and serve.

If kids are helping, transfer the crust to a cutting board after cooking both sides, let them help scatter on the toppings, and return the pizza to the grill to finish cooking.

From Countertop to Pizza Stone

A pizza peel is the most convenient tool for transferring a freshly topped pizza round from the kitchen counter to a pizza stone in the oven. The peel has only to be dusted with cornmeal or a little flour before the dough is stretched and placed on its broad surface. Then, the pizza should be transferred from the peel to the heated stone in the oven with a few swift jerks. Always handy, the peel can then be used as a giant spatula to move the cooked pizza to a cutting board.

In the absence of a pizza peel, a rimless baking sheet can be used to transfer the topped dough from the pizza stone to the oven. Because they are aluminum and not as slippery as thin, polished wood, you may need additional cornmeal or flour to transfer the pizza from the baking sheet to the pizza stone. You can use a conventional baking sheet by turning it over if you don't have a rimless one. Using tongs or a spatula, carefully lift and slide the hot pizza back onto the baking pan to cool.

Stretching the dough and placing it on 12-inch squares of parchment paper can make the journey to the oven a breeze when making individual pizzas. The parchment paper can be used to slip the pizza onto the stone by elevating it by the sides, or it can be placed directly on the stone. Even though more stability is required, this method can be used for pizzas of any size.

Whichever method you use, remember: Always open the oven and pull the oven rack and pizza stone out halfway before lifting your pizza from the kitchen counter—it's just plain safer than trying to do it with an uncooked pizza in your hand.

The dough becomes stickier if it overheats or is over-handled during the assembly process. Refrigerate it briefly (about 10 minutes), and it will become less "grabby." A quick cooling-off period will make it more cooperative and able to slide smoothly and cohesively into the oven.

Types of Cooking

There are various oven types when it comes to pizza cooking. The oldest is the traditional wood-burning oven, which was very common before the gas and electric oven. The wood-burning oven was there when pizza was birthed.

Wood-burning oven

The experience was needed in using the wood-burning oven because managing the wood was challenging. There was no thermometer to check the temperature in this kind of oven. Instead, people would rely on the refractory walls and their color. At the start, the color of the oven (cold oven) would be dark, then turn to almost red, and finally turn white when the ideal temperature was reached. The ideal temperature for cooking a classic pizza using a wood oven is 450° - 485°, and the time for cooking is about 1 minute and 30 seconds for Neapolitan pizza. The mouth's relationship with the chamber's overall volume is significant. The baker's pizza-cooking skill came in here because the filling had to be cooked in "oven mouth" to melt the mozzarella inside, combining it with the rest of the ingredients and ensuring that the pizza was not burnt. The wood consumption varies between 4-5 kg every hour. Another problem with this type of oven is that it needs lots of space to be installed.

Electric oven

Electric ovens vary depending on the model. Using a static electric oven for a pizzeria is recommended where the air naturally circulates and is not forced out. Convention through the lower cooking surface is the main system of cooking. Radiation is also part of cooking, whereby the upper resistances emit heat. There is also further cooking by heating the oven air. It is the type of oven used in rotisserie pizzerias. Due to its simplicity of use, even a person without much experience can operate this oven.

Gas ovens

These ovens are the same as wood ovens and static ones used for pizzerias. The pros of gas ovens are that you can quickly regulate the temperature, have a shorter heating period, are more hygienic, and have cheaper consumption than previous ones. With the burner invention, the gas ovens are increasingly used in pizzerias because the equipment under the cooking chamber heats upwards from the bottom. The burner makes the floor heat up more than chamber's ceiling.

Analyzing the three ovens, some chefs like the wood oven because they have the required skills to manage it.

With the tricks of a chef, the gas oven can make a pizza almost the same as the one made using a wood oven. However, there are course differences that are not easily noticeable.

The electric oven does not convince many people because the dough turns out too dry, making it lose its softness and hydration. However, this is just some people's view, and others like it very much.

CHAPTER 2: TIPS AND TRICKS

Heat up correctly: A good, crisp crust can only be achieved by baking in a very hot oven, which takes time. Therefore, start preheating the oven (and the pizza stone, if you're using one) at least 30 minutes before you plan to bake the pizza, but ideally for an hour.

Cruise it out: Using a rolling pin, the dough is worked from the center to the edges uniformly and effectively. Roll the dough quickly, turn it a quarter to the right, and do it again. Children that have trouble forming their hands properly can benefit greatly from this method. The dough must be rolled out as thinly as possible.

Earn further: Kids should know not to handle the dough too much, but they usually can't help themselves. Get the most out of the good times by fostering a spirit of experimentation and making allowances for inevitable setbacks. Don't risk supper by letting the kids play with the dough right before it's time to eat; instead, have a few extra balls on hand.

Try to contain your excitement: It's tempting to pile on every delicious topping imaginable when making pizza, but the crust and your taste buds can only take so much. We recommend keeping the number of toppings on each pie to a maximum of three.

A Gift Cake? To ensure that astronauts on long-duration space trips are well-fed, NASA has invented a 3-D printer that can produce pizza. The machine can make an entire pie in 70 seconds and shower it with flavor, aroma, and even micronutrients, as stated on the NASA website.

Get the proportions just right: Aim for a little of everything in each meal, and don't worry about sophisticated arithmetic formulae. The pizza toppings should be arranged in a single layer over the cheese, with minimum overlap. After removing the pizzas from the oven, top them with freshly chopped or torn herbs and a pinch of freshly ground black pepper. The pizza's scent will make it taste as pizza professionals have made it.

Put it down and take a break: Your pizza just came out of the oven, so please wait a few minutes before cutting it. This will give the cheese time to "set," preventing it from melting all over the pizza and making the toppings fall off in the middle of your bite.

Ensure you are utilizing the appropriate type of flour. Having strong flour is crucial for a lengthy leavening time.

Keep the yeast away from any salt: Yeast's activity is sanitized by salt, which is a disinfectant.

Calorie count of the water: The water temperature shouldn't be too high. Heat sterilization of the yeast is planned. Cold water works just as well.

Container: Pizza should be spread in a particular container. Due to its thick base, the oven tray should not be used to cook food.

Refrain from using a rolling pin: While a rolling pin is great for breaking the bubbles that leaven the dough and making it crumbly and light, using your hands to spread the pizza is the best way to ensure even cooking and a crispy crust.

A high-quality oven is required for pizza preparation.

In order to have the best possible pizza, you need to shape it by hand. Avoid using a rolling pin if you want a perfectly thin crust. Proofed dough can be felt when stretched by hand.

If the dough is shrinking and reshaping itself on the peel, give it five minutes for the gluten to relax, then gently stretch it again. I don't care much about the shape, as both round and oval have the same flavor, but thickness is important. I want the odds of winning to be as low as feasible.

Use sparingly when topping pizzas with sauce and toppings. Dough that contains heavy, wet ingredients steams rather than bouncing back to life. Uncooked, soggy pie is unacceptable.

Successfully close out the race. Put some chopped garlic in an olive oil-covered ramekin and leave it on your work counter. To add flavor and gloss to the dough, brush the cooked pizza with garlic oil as the last step.

Pizzas are at their finest when baked in a hot, bright oven with a fully engaged fire and rolling flames over the dome. If there is no flame in the fireplace, add a thin split log and wait for it to catch fire before proceeding with the pie.

Most ovens will reduce floor temperature after 10–15 pizzas. Rake the embers back over the floor and let it sit for 10 minutes to reheat the floor before using it. Sweep the floor again and return to making crisp pies after pushing the fire away, adding a thin log to the embers, and letting it light.

Some ingredients must be cooked before topping a raw pizza; they won't properly finish in the short amount of time the dough spends in the oven. Precook thinly sliced vegetables such as potatoes and eggplant. Other ingredients, such as greens and mushrooms, can contain a lot of water and should also be precooked, so they don't weigh down your pizza.

CHAPTER 3: EQUIPMENT AND TOOLS

Food Processor

Every time, a fast spin followed by a few minutes of hand kneading yields a smooth, elastic dough—bankable results.

KitchenAid Mixer

Another tried-and-true method for mixing ingredients and easily kneading them into a lukewarm, yeasty dough. A stand mixer like a KitchenAid that comes equipped with a dough hook can combine and knead dough just as effectively and reliably as a food processor.

Pizza Peel

The peel, which resembles a long spatula with a razor-thin cutting edge, is used to safely and easily carry pizza. The dough may be stretched and rolled out on its large surface, sauced and topped, then safely delivered to the hot oven. All it takes to become a master at removing dough from a peel is a little practice.

Pizza Stone or Pizza Steel

To simulate the ceramic floor of a wood-burning brick oven, either a pizza stone or steel is prepared beside the oven. The dough crisps up wonderfully on the heating stone. Pizza stones, which are hefty and frequently heated, may remain indefinitely on the bottom shelf of your oven. To get pies on and off the stone, use a peel or rimless baking sheet.

Rimless Baking Sheet

A rimless baking sheet can be used in place of a pizza stone and peel while preparing pizza. It's more adaptable than round-rimmed pizza pans since it serves as both a cooking area and a pizza peel, and the best thing is that you presumably already have one. Stretch and form the dough on the sheet pan, cook the pizza on it, and then move the piping-hot pizza onto a wooden cutting board to slice and serve. If you have two, you can cook two pizzas at once, which is a major time saver.

Wheel Slicer

Similar to how a great ice cream scoop feels in your hand and makes the job easier, Similar to how a wheel slicer enhances pizza consumption.

Bench Scraper

This magnificent, inexpensive professional tool helps lift the sticky dough and clean floured surfaces. Also It acts as a knife to divide dough balls into two or four pieces.

Pans

Most non-commercial pizza bakers wouldn't know what to buy when it comes to pans and other tools for making great pizza, and neither did I, without much trial and error.

Electronic Scale

Inexpensive ones are available that measure ounces and grams. For weighing flour and dough, ounces down to the tenth place works fine. However, if you are making Italian sausage at home, look for a more accurate scale that measures in grams to the hundredth place.

Serving Trays or Cardboard Pizza Circles

If you serve your pizza on an aluminum tray, be sure it is warmed, or put a parchment layer between the pizza and the tray, so the bottom of the crust doesn't sweat and get soggy. Another option is ready-made cardboard circles.

Rolling Pins

A standard wood or aluminum rolling pin will work to roll out the dough balls. Using the cutter pans for your thin-crust pizza, you will also want a small rolling pin to trim the excess dough from the cutter pan.

Food Processor or Stand Mixer

You can also mix the dough by hand. I suggest getting the processor if you don't already have either mixer. It costs significantly less and happens much faster.

Dough Docker

This tool is a short-handled roller with metal or plastic spines and can be used to poke (dock) holes in raw. Roll the dough before it is baked to prevent bubbling.

CHAPTER 4: METHODS AND PIZZA DOUGH RECIPES

The Dough

There is no such thing as perfect dough: there are many, each with its own strengths. Some bake up extra crisp, others have tangy flavors, and some produce perfectly smooth pizzas, while others are airier, with giant bubbles that puff up in the oven. So whether you're looking for a quick-rise recipe for weeknights or an artisanal-style dough that requires a little more attention, you'll find just the thing in this chapter to fit your family's routine and pizza-night style.

Making pizza at home is a surprisingly simple process that becomes more simple (and addictive) with practice. Begin by selecting a dough that meets your current needs, and then branch out and try the others once you've mastered one. Some of these recipes can be prepared in advance and frozen or refrigerated for optimal convenience. I've included these instructions and other tips and tricks whenever possible to help make pizza night a fun and rewarding experience for everyone.

Doughs that don't require aging have never piqued my interest. Aging gives food body, texture, and flavor. The perfect crust requires some forethought, but once you get there, you can't help but enjoy the process. Once you realize how easy this process is, you will quickly get over your pre-planning jitters.

Most dough recipes are far complicated, take too long to prepare, and produce poor results. Additionally, you won't find any dough recipes here if you're looking for a diversity. However, one very easy and precise dough mix, in my view, will give a great, brown, delicious, crispy crust for the numerous varieties of pizza. Regardless, the flavors will change based to the pans used.

Consider buying professional pre-made crusts if you don't want to meddle with the most vital aspect of the pizza. If you buy premade pizza crust, you'll pay almost as much as if you made the whole pizza from scratch, and you won't even get the same quality of pizza. Preservatives and conditioners for the dough are included in the premade crust to extend its shelf life, but they don't add much to the taste.

A store-bought crust and my homemade dough recipe cannot be compared.

We can prepare dough in a food processor, which is the quickest method and what I recommend. A good food processor will cost between $60 and $70. There are more expensive devices available if desired, but they should not be required. A 12-cup food processor is ideal for my dough recipe. Although a 10-cup will suffice, it is insufficient, and a 14-cup is excessive. Hamilton Beach is what I use.

A stand mixer, such as a KitchenAid, is another mechanical alternative. They cost about $200. They are not only more expensive than a food processor, but they also take a lot longer to blend.

Then there's the hand-kneading method, which older generations used to make bread three times a week for their huge families. If you're going to mix by hand and haven't worked with yeast doughs before, consult a cookbook, conduct some internet study, or ask a bread-making buddy to demonstrate how to combine and knead bread ingredients by hand.

My "easy" dough recipe:

- 17 oz bread flour (about 3 1/2 cup)
- 1/2 teaspoon instant (rapid rise) 10 oz. chilly (80 °F—to the touch) yeast 1 1/4 cup tap water

My basic dough recipe consists of flour, water, and yeast, but let's take a closer look at each ingredient.

Flour

Bread flour is suggested. Its greater protein level results in a stronger dough and crispier crust, although regular all-purpose flour would suffice. The crust will be softer as a result. You may experiment with several brands and stay with the one you like most, although they tend to be rather similar. You could simply shop by price.

Yeast

Most dough recipes call for active dry yeast, but rehydrating it takes time and is unnecessary. Instead, I prefer instant (rapid-rise) yeast, which may be blended with flour and water straight. In the end, you won't notice any difference, but you'll save yourself a lot of unneeded monkeying.

4-ounce jars of instant yeast are common. Although one jar should provide around 64 batches of dough, it is expensive in that quantity. A jar costs between $8 and $10. Instant yeast is also available in three-pack sachets, with each package containing around 4 12 tablespoons of yeast. That will make 4 batches of dough and will cost between $1.60 and $1.75. It's the same price as the jar. Some supermarkets sell it in vacuum-sealed 1-pound packets for less than $5. SAF-Instant, my personal favorite, is available for purchase online. Fill a storage container halfway with the contents, place it in the freezer, and take out tiny amounts as needed. If you have active dry yeast, use it entirely before switching to instant.

Although we only used fresh (cake) yeast at the bakery, I didn't see any benefit to utilizing fresh yeast in pizza dough. Any yeast will do, but instant yeast involves the least amount of effort. If you want to use cake yeast, 14 ounces is sufficient. Simply dissolve it in water, stir it around, and combine it with the flour.

Water

The water in New York pizza crusts is said to be excellent. I wasn't impressed with New York pizza, and I'm not sure what the crust is all about. If the "excellent water" argument is correct, how come my favorite pizza of all time has the best crust and the worst city water I've ever tasted? Their water was highly chlorinated, and my mentor did not filter it. You may experiment with softened or unsoftened, filtered or unfiltered, and discover what you like. In other words, the taste of water is not the most important consideration. The main issues are quantity and temperature.

A scale is quite useful in this situation. There are variations among measuring cups, I've found. One cup of water, for example, weighs 8 ounces, and we need 10 ounces for a single dough batch. That quantity should fit on the 14 measuring line, however not all cups are correctly "lined." So, first weigh your water and observe where 10 ounces falls on your cup. It might be slightly over or below the 14 cup mark. You will have to rely on trial and error if you don't have a scale. It's important to use the right amount!

Another factor is the water's temperature. It should be chilly enough to touch (80 °F). Excessively hot water may destroy the yeast. If the dough is warm, it will rise faster; if it is cold, it will rise more slowly.

High altitude pizza

The facts about salt, sugar, and oil.

I don't like "thick and chewy" crusts, but if that's what you want, the fundamental recipe will need to be tweaked. Add a teaspoon each of salt, sugar, and yeast, and combine. Salt tenderizes the dough while also significantly slowing fermentation. Both are undesirable features in my opinion, and I do not want either in my pizza dough.

If no salt is added to the dough formula, the dough must be worked cold, no more than an hour after it has been removed from the refrigerator. When the dough heats up, it might become sticky and difficult to manage. Of course, if you're adding salt for taste or a more soft crust, the temperature is irrelevant. Salt tenderizes the dough, making it less sticky and resulting in a stronger dough.

The final work will eventually inform you what to include and exclude. When you smell the crust after baking your pizza, you will smell the purity of an unadulterated excellent crust. When you dine out, do the same sniff test; it won't be long until you quit dining and remain at home producing better pizzas and enjoying them more.

Sugar has little flavoring effect on the dough unless you prepare a sweet dough, such as cinnamon rolls, and use a lot of it. Sugar performs two things: it feeds the yeast, causing the dough to rise, and it helps to brown the crust. When there is no salt in the recipe, it is unnecessary to add sugar to help in the rising process, and your crust will brown perfectly without it.

To soften the dough, add a tablespoon or two of your preferred oil. You never heard anything about olive oil in the past, at least not that I was aware of, and now that's all you hear. Keep in mind that some oils, such as olive oil and sesame seeds, may impart their own tastes to the completed dish. That's OK if that's what you want. Most pizza places use vegetable oil or a solid shortening to soften the dough, but please start with my basic recipe. It's possible that you'll want to go even further.

If you do experiment with oil, some experts recommend not adding it to the water but rather waiting until the dough begins to mix. However, oil and water do not mix.

Dough made from wheat

To be considered whole wheat, you must use 100% whole wheat flour, which does not function well. It is gluten-free and has a weak, dry crust. Instead, for a great dough, use just 1/3 to 12 whole wheat flour and the rest white bread flour. In fact, that mixture is easier to work with and roll out than pure white flour. The mixing instructions for wheat flour are the same as for all white flour.

Using a stand mixer to make dough

Using a stand mixer, the actual mixing time is around 10 minutes from the moment the ingredients begin to combine.

Before you begin, measure all the ingredients. To make the dough, add the water to the mixer bowl, throw in the flour and instant yeast, twist in the dough hook, twist and lock the bowl onto the mixer, lower and lock the motor head, and mix on the second speed until the ingredients are incorporated.

10 minutes of 10-second speed mixing. Stop the mixer, elevate the head, and press the ball of dough down if the dough climbs the hook or isn't gripping on the hook. Relock the head and continue kneading until the dough has been kneaded for the entire 10 minutes. Using the stand mixer, you can create slightly under a double batch. 2 cups (16 ounces) water, 27 ounces flour, and 1 teaspoon yeast for the bigger batch When finished, you will have 43 ounces of dough.

Remove the finished dough from the mixer. The dough should not adhere to your fingertips at this point. If it does, add a tablespoon of flour to the mixer and knead until the flour is entirely integrated. If necessary, repeat. If the dough is too firm, add a tablespoon of water and knead it again until it is just perfect. Form a ball and place it in a big plastic food storage bag to keep it cool.

Mixing the dough using a food processor

Most people don't realize that a food processor can be used to mix yeast dough, but making pizza dough in one of these high-speed machines is the easiest and fastest way to get your pizza on the table.

Measure out the flour, water, and yeast; combine the flour and yeast in a mixing dish, then add water on top. Replace the lid and press the high-speed button. If your measurements are correct, the dough should come together fast. When it begins to blend, continue to process at high speed for around 15 seconds.

The mixing time is irrelevant until the components begin to draw together into a ball. That is when you begin timing. When the dough has combined visually and physically, the food processor will increase its speed.

Remove the top and press the dough down closer to the blade if it does not combine after half a minute. Keep an eye out for consistency. If it's too sticky, add one tablespoon of flour. You should add one tablespoon of water if the mixture is too dry. Return the cover, then carry on with processing. Repeat the process if the issue persists. Dough that is either too dry or too moist will not mix well. Only practice will teach you how excellent dough should feel.

The food processor motor might burn out if the dough is excessively firm (too dry). While mixing, you will hear it groan. The tough dough is also more difficult to roll out. A scale for ingredients is essential!

Remove the ball and blade from the processing bowl after 15 seconds of mixing the dough. Remember that the blade is very sharp. If any dough adheres to it, simply contact the pieces with the final ball of dough, and they will peel away. "Round up" the dough ball as described below and refrigerate it in a big plastic food storage bag.

Remember to clean the machine as soon as the dough is soft. Rinse the interior of the blade, then set it back in the bowl and fill it with soap and hot water to soften it. After that, rinse the lid with hot water, then wipe the blade with a toothbrush and wash the bowl with a dish pad after about 5 minutes. Keep the blade away from your fingertips! Cleaning the machine might take as long as making the dough, but it just takes a few minutes.

Rounding up the dough ball

Once the materials are combined into a rough ball, use both hands to "round it up" into a smooth, tight ball by pulling the edges from outside to inside numerous times.

The dough will be considerably warmer in parts than in others. Continue to bring the dough under until it is combined with the colder portion. Pinch the bottom seam securely together after the fabric has been tucked into a neat ball. (If the dough is excessively moist and sticky, it will be difficult to manage when formed into balls and rolled out.)

Seal each dough ball in a big food storage bag and lay it seam-side down in the refrigerator on a dish towel or other cloth surface. This will limit the amount of chilling on the bottom of the dough. If your fridge has wire shelves, place a plate or a flat surface beneath the dough ball.

You might want to make two or three batches of dough, depending on your situation. Remember that one batch creates three medium pizzas or two extra-large pizzas, so it's simple to prepare.

Refrigerate dough balls on a cloth to keep their bottoms from chilling. Different colored twist ties indicate each ball's weight, which corresponds to the size of pizza produced by each.

Giving the dough balls time to rise

After letting the dough rest in the fridge for a full day, divide it into three 9-ounce balls or two 13-ounce balls and let it rise again until it has doubled in size. To separate the dough balls, write on zipper closure bags or use different colored twist ties, such as white for tiny, red for medium, and green for extra-large.

Return the dough to the refrigerator to prove for another 24 hours. An ice-cold refrigerator may chill the yeast to the point that the dough does not rise. If this is the case, try slightly warmer water next time and raise the yeast to one teaspoon. Another useful suggestion is to let the dough remain at room temperature for a few hours before putting it in the refrigerator.

The bottom line of the proving stage is that it makes rolling out the dough balls simpler. You must have air bubbles in them or you will be battling a dead horse. If the dough is difficult to roll, let it prove for a longer period of time the following time. Many excellent things happen throughout the aging process, which is essential for superb taste and crust. Don't be discouraged. Handling dough in this manner takes less time than it appears. It simply takes a minute or two to round them up as they age, and the payoff far outweighs the effort.

Pizzerias would struggle to roll out their dough if they did not use a similar proving procedure. The only change in a commercial venture is that most of the dough balls are devoured right once, and what remains is re-rolled once again.

Some businesses, such as Domino's, get proofed dough balls in cartons from their commissary and are ready to go. They do not use an electric roller, but instead push the dough out with their fingertips. Others make the dough spin in the air. It all leads to the same result, which is known as sheeting the dough.

We have the time at home to prepare our pizzas the way Pizza Hut did in the beginning, by rolling them out from fresh dough baked on-site.

In terms of shelf life, pizza dough differs greatly from other yeast doughs. It will stay in the refrigerator for ten days or longer provided the dough balls are handled carefully. Here are some things that most amateur pizza makers, as well as some professionals, don't know. Assume you created your dough Monday night, let it rest for a day, and then divided it into three smaller dough balls for three medium pizzas on Tuesday night. Then, if they rise for another day, three dough balls will be ready to roll out on Wednesday.

Rolling out the Dough

There isn't much to know about rolling out a dough ball, but you do need to know a few key things, which I'll go over with you.

You're ready to roll out a dough ball for any of the pizza types you're creating once your dough has risen a couple of times and your dough balls are properly proofed. Because we don't roll them out as thinly, the deep dish, garlic strips, pan style, and square pan are simpler to roll out.

Begin by wearing short-sleeved shirts whenever you're in the kitchen, and don't forget to wear a hat. I see cooks with long sleeves, occasionally rolled up, even on high-end TV shows, so why not start the proper way?

After washing your countertop with a disinfecting cleanser and clean hands, lightly dust the area where you will roll out the dough with flour. Next, place the dough ball on the floured surface and add more flour to the top. Don't worry about how much you use; the dough will absorb as much as it can without sticking to your hands or equipment. With your hand, press all the air out of the dough.

When you press down on the dough ball, the air should whoosh out and the dough ball should be completely flat. If the dough does not smooth out, it has not relaxed sufficiently and will be more difficult to deal with. If your dough balls did not rise as much as they should, it's possible that you didn't give them enough time or that your refrigerator is too cold. Allow them to warm up for 2 to 3 hours before putting them back in the fridge to chill down again before rolling. Unless you add salt, the dough must always be chilled when dealing with. The unsalted dough at room temperature might be sticky. After a few sessions with the dough, you'll know how it should look and feel before rolling.

Pick up the dough and distribute additional flour on the counter, assuming the dough ball is deflated and ready to go. Put the dough back on the floured board and add extra flour. Roll the dough out to the desired size using your rolling pin. Stop rolling if it resists you and refuses to roll any farther. You're not going to win that one!

Lift the dough once more, re-spread the flour over the counter and top, and set aside for 5 to 10 minutes. The dough will readily roll out the rest of the way when it has relaxed. Of course, you'll want your oven, pans, sauces, and other ingredients ready before you begin rolling out the dough balls, but while it's resting, you may discover something else that has to be done.

After rolling out the ball to the correct size, use the bench brush to brush the excess flour off both sides of the dough. It is now ready to bake in any pan style you like. If you're baking on a stone (without a pan), I recommend brushing off the top and lightly shaking off the bottom. A little flour on the bottom side will help it slip off the wood peel more easily.

CHAPTER 5: 105 RECIPES

(ALSO INCLUDES SWEET PIZZA)

1. New York Style Pizza

Preparation time: 10 minutes
Cooking time: 15 minutes
Servings: 4

Ingredients:

- 1 teaspoon dynamic dry yeast
- 2/3 cup warm water (110 °F/45 °C)
- 2 cups regular flour
- 1 teaspoon salt
- 2 tablespoons olive oil
- 1 (10-ounce) tomato sauce
- 1 pound squashed mozzarella cheddar
- 1/2 cup ground Romano cheddar
- 1/4 cup hacked new basil
- 1 tablespoon dried oregano
- 1 teaspoon red pepper chips
- 2 tablespoons olive oil

Directions:

1. Sprinkle the yeast over the outer layer of the warm water in a huge bowl. Let stand for 1 moment, then mix to squashed.
2. Blend in the flour, salt, and olive oil. When the dough is too thick even to consider mixing, turn it out onto a floured surface, and massage for 5 minutes.
3. Massage in somewhat more flour, assuming that the dough is excessively tacky. Put the dough in an oiled basin, cover, and let it rise in a hot place until it has increased in size.
4. Preheat the broiler to 475 °F (245 °C). In the case of utilizing a pizza stone, preheat it in the broiler, too, setting it on the most minimal rack.
5. At the point when the dough has risen, smooth it out on a daintily floured surface. Roll or loosen up into a 12-inch circle and put on a baking pan. If you are utilizing a pizza stone, put it on a piece of material while preheating the stone on the stove.
6. Spread the pureed tomatoes equally over the dough. Then, sprinkle with

oregano, mozzarella cheddar, basil, Romano cheddar, and red pepper chips.

7. Prepare for 12 to 15 minutes in the preheated broiler until the lower part of the crust is seared. The cheddar is melted and effervescent when you lift the edge a bit.

8. Cool for around 5 minutes before cutting and serving.

2. Butternut Squash Pizzas with Rosemary

Preparation time: 10 minutes
Cooking time: 30 minutes
Servings: 4

Ingredients:

- 1 (16 ounces) package of pizza crust dough
- One cup of thinly sliced onion
- 2 tablespoons grated Asiago cheese
- 1 teaspoon fresh rosemary
- 1/2 butternut squash
- 3 tablespoons of olive oil
- 1 tablespoon cornmeal
- Salt and black pepper

Directions:

1. Preheat oven to 400°F.
2. In a roasting pan, combine the diced butternut squash and sliced onion. Season with salt, black pepper, chopped rosemary, and 2 tablespoons of olive oil. Toss to coat.
3. Roast the squash mixture in the oven for 20 minutes or until tender.
4. Meanwhile, on a floured surface, roll each dough ball into an 8-inch circle. Place the dough rounds on a baking sheet dusted with cornmeal (you may need 2 baking sheets depending on their size).
5. Once the squash mixture is roasted, distribute it evenly over the two dough rounds. Sprinkle the grated Asiago cheese and the remaining 1 tablespoon of olive oil on top.
6. Bake the pizzas in the oven for 10-12 minutes or until the crust is golden brown.
7. Cut each pizza into quarters and serve.

3. Cajun Shrimp and Scallop Pizza

Preparation time: 10 minutes
Cooking time: 30 minutes
Servings: 8

Ingredients:

- 1 15-oz pizza dough, store-bought
- 10 oz shrimp, peeled and deveined
- 14 oz scallops, cleaned and rinsed
- 1 cup white mushrooms, quartered
- 3 shallots, sliced
- 4 garlic cloves, chopped
- 1 cup dried parsley flakes
- ½ cup mozzarella
- ½ cup pizza sauce
- ½ cup all-purpose cream
- 3 tbsp olive oil
- 1 ½ tsp Cajun seasoning
- Salt and black pepper to taste

Directions:

1. Preheat the oven to 450 °F.
2. Prepare the ingredients and place them in separate bowls.
3. Use a large skillet and boil 3 tablespoons of olive oil over high heat.
4. Sauté garlic until golden brown; add the shallots.
5. After 2 minutes, add the mushrooms, then continue sautéing for 5 minutes.
6. Add scallops, then the shrimp. Add the Cajun seasoning.
7. Pour cooking cream. Remove from the heat and put aside to cool.
8. Grease the baking pan and stretch the dough to a round or rectangular shape.
9. Pour and spread pizza sauce evenly on the dough, leaving a little space for the crust.
10. Top with the Cajun seafood mix using a spoon.
11. Add grated mozzarella cheese; spread it generously throughout the dough and bake for 20 minutes until the cheese bubbles.
12. Let it cool down a bit. Slice and serve.

4. Caramel Apple Pizza

Preparation time: 10 minutes
Cooking time: 1 hour and 5 minutes
Servings: 3

Ingredients:

For the Cookie Crust:

- 3 cups all-purpose flour + 1 tsp.
- 2 lightly packed brown sugar
- 3/4 tsp baking powder
- 1 cup kosher salt
- 1 cup (2 sticks) softened butter
- 1/2 cup granulated sugar

For the Toppings:

- Pinch kosher salt
- 8 oz. block of cream cheese
- 4 tbsp softened butter
- 1/2 cup powdered sugar
- 2 large apples, chopped
- 1/2 cup chopped pecans
- 1/2 tsp ground cinnamon
- 1/4 cup caramel
- 1 tsp pure vanilla extract

Directions:

1. In a huge bowl, whisk together the heating powder, flour, and salt.
2. In another huge bowl, a hand blender beat spread and sugar until cushioned and pale in shading. Include egg and vanilla and beat until consolidated, including flour blend steadily until completely joined. Shape it into a circle and enclose it with plastic. Refrigerate for 60 minutes.
3. When prepared to heat, preheat the broiler to 350ºF and fix a vast preparing sheet with material paper. At that point, oil with a cooking splash. On a gently floured surface, turn batter into a 12-inch circle. Spot batter on arranged preparing sheet and heat until set, yet somewhat delicate, around 25 minutes. Let cool totally.

In the meantime, make besting:

1. In an enormous bowl utilizing a hand blender, beat cream cheddar and spread until smooth.
2. Include powdered sugar and beat until no lumps stay at that point, including vanilla, cinnamon, and a salt spot.

3. Ice the outside layer with cream cheddar icing. Then, top with apples, walnuts, and a sprinkle of caramel.

5. Caramelized Onions and Ricotta Cheese Pizza

Preparation time: 10 minutes
Cooking time: 35 minutes
Servings: 4

Ingredients:

For the Crust:

- 2 cups grated mozzarella cheese
- 2 tbsp dairy-free cream cheese, room temperature
- 2 large eggs, beaten
- ⅓ cup almond flour
- 1 tsp dried Italian seasoning

For the Toppings:

- Salt to taste
- 2 tbsp butter
- 2 red onions
- 1 cup crumbled ricotta cheese
- 1 tbsp almond milk
- 1 cup fresh curly endive, chopped

Directions:

1. First preheat the oven to 425 °F and grease a circular pizza pan.
2. Combine the mozzarella cheese and dairy-free cream cheese in a microwave-safe bowl and melt in the microwave for 1 minute.
3. Remove from the oven and mix in the eggs, almond flour, and Italian seasoning.
4. Spread the dough on the pizza pan and bake in the oven for 6 minutes or until golden brown and crusty.
5. Meantime, melt the butter, in a large pan, mix in the onions. Reduce the temperature to low, sprinkle the onions with salt and black pepper, and simmer, turning often, for 15 to 20 minutes, or until caramelized. Increase the heat.
6. In a medium dish, add the almond milk and ricotta cheese and spread it over the crust. Serve with the caramelized onions on top.
7. Bake for 10 minutes, then remove from the oven.
8. Serve the pizza warm, topped with the curly endive.

6. Caramelized Onions Pizza

Preparation time: 10 minutes
Cooking time: 50 minutes
Servings: 8

Ingredients:

For the Caramelized Onions:

- 2 tbsp olive oil
- 1/4 tsp salt
- 1/4 cup mayonnaise
- 2 tbsp cashew milk (unsweetened)
- 1 cup white onion, sliced
- 1 tbsp nutritional yeast (optional)

For the crust:

- 2 cups almond flour
- 1/2 cup coconut flour
- 1/2 tsp Italian seasoning
- 1/2 tsp salt
- 4 eggs whites
- 1 tbsp baking powder
- 1/4 cup avocado oil
- 1/4 cup cashew milk (unsweetened)

Garnish (optional):

- Fresh basil
- Ground pepper

Directions:

1. Prepare the caramelized onions:
    a. Cook the onions in olive oil.
    b. Sprinkle with salt.
    c. Cook for 15-20 minutes or until the potatoes are tender and golden in color.
    d. Set aside.
2. Prepare the sauce: Whisk all the sauce ingredients until you get a smooth consistency. Set aside.
3. Prepare the crust: Whisk all the dry ingredients for the crust in a bowl. Then, add the wet ingredients and stir until a sticky ball of dough forms.
4. Divide the dough into 2.
5. Brush a big piece of parchment paper with oil. Turn the 1st piece of dough into the parchment paper and form it into a disk.
6. Cover the dough with parchment and use a rolling pin to roll it into a 10-inch circle. Do the same with the other piece of dough. Discard the top parchment paper.
7. Set the dough (and the bottom parchment paper) on a baking sheet. Bake for 20-25 minutes until the crust is firm and the edges are golden brown.
8. Put the pizza sauce on the pizza. Top with the caramelized onions. Bake for 5 to 8 minutes.
9. Garnish with chopped fresh basil and freshly ground pepper, if desired.

7. Cast Iron Fennel Pizza

Preparation time: 10 minutes
Cooking time: 55 minutes
Servings: 2

Ingredients:

- 12-ounce pizza crust dough, prepared
- 5 tbsp. of oil, olive
- 8 ounces of Italian sausage, sweet – remove the casings
- Salt, kosher
- 1/3 cup of marinara sauce, prepared
- 3/4 cup of mozzarella cheese, low-moisture, grated coarsely
- ½ thin-sliced bulb of fennel, small
- 3 thin-sliced cloves of garlic

To Serve:

- Basil leaves, torn
- Crushed pepper flakes, red

Directions:

1. Place the rack in the uppermost part of the oven—preheat the oven to 475 °F.
2. on a clean work surface place the dough . Drizzle with a tablespoon of oil and turn to coat. Stretch to 10-inches around and loosely cover with cling wrap.
3. Heat 1 tablespoon of oil in a large-sized, cast-iron skillet on medium heat. Cook the sausage and break it into small-sized pieces till browned and fully cooked for five to eight minutes. Place the sausage in a small-sized bowl.
4. Remove the skillet from the stovetop burner. Remove cling wrap and lay dough inside carefully. Season as desired and spread the marinara sauce over the whole dough surface. Top the pizza with mozzarella cheese, fennel, cooked sausage, and garlic. Drizzle with 2 tablespoons more oil.
5. Transfer the skillet to your oven. Bake on the top rack till crust edges turn golden brown. Cheese should be bubbly and browned here and there for 10 to 14 minutes or so. Allow to cool for five minutes, and top with basil and pepper flakes. Drizzle with the last tablespoon of oil and serve.

8. Cauliflower-Spinach Pizza

Preparation time: 10 minutes
Cooking time: 30 minutes
Servings: 2

Ingredients:

Crust:

- 1 cauliflower, finely chopped
- 1 egg
- 100 g mozzarella cheese (grated)
- ½ tsp salt
- ¼ tsp pepper
- ½ tsp dried oregano

Toppings:

- ¾ cup mozzarella cheese, shredded
- ¼ cup pecorino Romano cheese, grated
- ½ cup cooked spinach
- A handful of sun-dried tomatoes, chopped

Directions:

1. Steam the cauliflower until they are soft.
2. Put the cooked cauliflower on a clean tea towel and gently press to remove all liquid. Getting rid of the liquid ensures that you will have a crisp pizza base.
3. Put the cauliflower in a large bowl. Combine the remaining ingredients, and thoroughly combine to create a ball.
4. Put your cauliflower "dough" on a paper-lined baking sheet and press to form a round pizza crust.
5. Spray some olive oil on top. Preheat the oven to 350 °F and bake for 15-20 minutes or until the crust is brown. Let the crust cool.
6. Sprinkle mozzarella cheese over the crust. Spread the spinach and tomatoes over the mozzarella cheese. Top with Pecorino Romano. Sprinkle a pinch of salt over the pizza.
7. Return the pizza to the oven for a further 5 minutes of baking to melt the cheese.

9. Cauliflower-Vegan Bacon Pizza Casserole

Preparation time: 10 minutes
Cooking time: 40 minutes
Servings: 4

Ingredients:

- 4 cups cauliflower rice
- 1 cup grated mozzarella cheese
- 1 tbsp dried thyme
- Salt and black pepper to taste

For the Toppings:

- ¼ cup sugar-free tomato sauce
- 1 cup grated mozzarella cheese
- ½ cup vegan bacon slices

Directions:

1. Preheat the oven to 425 °F and gently oil a baking dish. Set aside.
2. Pour the cauliflower rice into a safe microwave bowl, mix in 1 tablespoon of water, and steam in the microwave for 1 minute.
3. Remove the bowl and mix the mozzarella cheese, thyme, salt, and black pepper. Pour the mixture into the baking dish, smooth it evenly, and bake for 5 minutes in the oven.
4. Take out the dish from the oven and spread the tomato sauce on top. Next, scatter the mozzarella cheese on the sauce and then arrange the vegan bacon slices on top.
5. Bake in the oven for 15 more minutes or until the cheese melts.
6. Remove the dish and serve the pizza casserole warm.

10. Chaffle Pizza

Preparation time: 10 minutes
Cooking time: 15 minutes
Servings: 2

Ingredients:

Batter:

- Coconut flour, 1 tsp
- Egg white, 1
- Mozzarella cheese, shredded, ½ cup
- Cream cheese, softened, 1 tsp
- Baking powder, ¼ tsp
- Italian seasoning, 1/8 tsp
- Garlic powder, 1/8 tsp
- Salt

Toppings:

- Marinara sauce (sugar-free), 3 tsp
- Pepperoni, 6 slices - cut in half to make 12 pieces
- Parmesan cheese, grated, 1 tbsp
- Mozzarella cheese, shredded, ½ cup
- Basil seasoning, ¼ tsp

Directions:

1. Preheat your oven to 400 °F. Plug in your waffle maker and preheat. Combine all the ingredients thoroughly to make the batter. Cook half of the batter in the waffle maker for 3 minutes or until the chaffle is done.
2. Gently take the cooked chaffle out of the waffle maker. Cook the second half of the batter. Top both chaffles with marinara sauce, pepperoni slices, and cheese. Bake in the oven for 5 minutes or until melting and the cheese bubbles. Top with basil seasoning.

11. Cheese and Almond Pizza

Preparation time: 10 minutes
Cooking time: 25 minutes
Servings: 4

Ingredients:

- Eggs (2)
- Alfredo sauce (1/2 cup)
- Cheddar cheese (4 ounces)
- Butter (5 tablespoons)
- Almond meal (1 cup)
- Stevia (1 ½ teaspoons)
- Garlic powder (1/2 teaspoon)
- Baking powder (1 ½ teaspoons)
- Thyme (1/4 teaspoon)
- Oregano (1/2 teaspoon)

Directions:

1. Spritz a pizza baking pan using cooking oil spray. Set the oven to 350ºF.
2. Combine the dry fixings and fold in the eggs. Melt and add the butter to the mixture.
3. Prepare the crust and spread it out evenly onto the pan. Cook the crust for 5 to 7 minutes. Transfer it from the oven and add the alfredo sauce.
4. Garnish it with cheese. Bake for another 5 to 7 minutes.
5. Serve when it's browned to your liking.

12. Cheese Crust Pizza

Preparation time: 10 minutes
Cooking time: 25 minutes
Servings: 2

Ingredients:

- 1 28-oz can unsweetened, peeled tomato
- ¼ cup extra-virgin olive oil
- Salt to taste
- 1 tbsp red wine vinegar
- 1 tsp dried oregano
- ½ tsp red pepper flakes
- ¼ tsp black pepper
- 6 oz. shredded mozzarella cheese
- 1 tsp dried parsley
- 5 oz cheese of your choice
- 1 tsp garlic powder
- 34 medium eggs
- 1 ½ oz pepperoni
- 1 tsp dried basil
- 1 tsp dried oregano

Directions:

1. Preheat the oven to 400 °F and line an oven pan with parchment paper or extra-virgin olive oil.
2. To begin your sauce, pour the peeled tomatoes, ½ cup of tomato liquid, and olive oil into a blender and puree. Add the vinegar, oregano, basil, parsley, garlic powder, red pepper flakes, black pepper, and salt, and mix well. Adjust the Ingredients: to taste.
3. Transfer to a sealable jar and store in the refrigerator.
4. Mix the eggs and 6 oz mozzarella in a bowl and stir well. Place your pizza base on the oven tray, forming two medium pizzas or 1 large pizza.
5. Bake the crust for 10 minutes.; Take from the oven and let it cool for 2 to 3 minutes. Then, increase the oven temperature to 450 °F.
6. Spread about 3 tbsp of tomato sauce over the crust and sprinkle with dried oregano. Add the pepperoni and cheese.
7. Bake for 5 to 10 minutes, ensuring the cheese gets a chance to melt and brown to your liking.
8. Serve as is or with a side salad.

13. Cheeseburger Pizza

Preparation time: 10 minutes
Cooking time: 20 minutes
Servings: 5

Ingredients:

For the Peel:

- 2 cups shredded mozzarella
- 2 tbsp cream cheese
- 1 egg
- ¾ cup almond flour

For the Toppings:

- ½ pound ground beef
- 1 tbsp Worcestershire sauce
- ½ tsp onion powder
- ½ tsp garlic powder
- ½ tsp salt
- ⅓ cup Thousand Island dressing
- One cup of shredded cheddar
- One cup of shredded mozzarella
- 1 tbsp sugar-free ketchup
- 1 tbsp mustard
- ½ cup dill pickle slices, drained

Directions:

For the peel:

1. Warm up the oven to 425 °F.
2. Microwave two cups of mozzarella and cream cheese in a microwave-safe bowl for one minute. Stir to combine, then return to microwave for another 30 seconds or until cheese has melted.
3. Combine the almond flour and egg in a mixing bowl.
4. Roll the dough out onto a large piece of parchment paper. Add a second piece of parchment on top.
5. Form a 12-inch-diameter circle out of the dough.
6. Replace the top piece of paper and transfer the dough to a pizza pan on the bottom sheet.
7. Bake for ten minutes till the peel is slightly golden.
8. For some extra sturdy peel that holds up well, attentively flip the peel over and prepare in the oven for 3 more minutes.

For the Toppings:

9. Whereas pizza peel is baking, brown the ground beef, crumbling this as this cooks. Drain the grease and spice with the Worcestershire sauce, onion powder, garlic powder, and salt. Stir well to mix.
10. Spread the Thousand Island dressing over the prepared pizza peel and top with the cheddar and mozzarella.
11. Spoon the prepared beef over the cheese. Drizzle with ketchup and mustard.
12. Return the pizza to the oven and prepare for ten minutes until the peel is golden or the cheese has softened.
13. Lay pickle slices over the pizza and cut it into 8 pieces.
14. Serve hot.

14. Cheesesteak Pizza

Preparation time: 10 minutes
Cooking time: 30 minutes
Servings: 8

Ingredients:

- 2 tablespoons olive oil, divided
- 8 oz. beef sirloin, sliced thinly
- 1 onion, sliced thinly
- 1 green bell pepper, sliced thinly
- 8 oz. mushrooms, sliced
- 20-inch pizza crust
- 12 slices white cheese
- 2 cups Mexican cheese blend, shredded

Directions:

1. Preheat your oven to 400 °F.
2. Add 1 tablespoon olive oil to a pan over medium heat.
3. Cook the beef while stirring for 4 to 5 minutes.
4. Add the beef to a plate lined with a paper towel.
5. Pour the remaining oil into the pan.
6. Cook the onion, bell pepper, and mushrooms for 5 minutes.
7. Add the pizza crust to a pizza pan.
8. Cover with white cheese slices.
9. Top with the beef and mushroom mixture.
10. Sprinkle the Mexican cheese blend on top—bake in the oven for 20 minutes.

15. Cheesy Garlic Pizza

Preparation time: 10 minutes
Cooking time: 2 minutes
Servings: 6 to 8

Ingredients:

- 1 refrigerated pizza crust
- 1 cup pizza sauce
- 2 tbsp minced garlic
- ¼ cup feta cheese, crumbled
- ¼ cup mozzarella cheese

Directions:

1. Spread the pizza sauce on top of the pizza crust.
2. Sprinkle the minced garlic and feta cheese on top.
3. Top with mozzarella cheese.
4. Bake inside the oven for 2 minutes.

16. Satay Pizza with Chicken

Preparation time: 10 minutes
Cooking time: 30 minutes
Servings: 4

Ingredients:

- Vegetable oil: 1 tbsp.
- Green onions (chopped): 1 bunch
- Pita bread: 4 inches (4 rounds)
- Chopped chicken (boneless and skinless): 2 breasts
- Peanut sauce: 1 cup
- Provolone cheese: 4 slices

Directions:

1. Sauté chicken in hot oil in one skillet for almost 7 minutes and keep it aside.
2. Preheat your oven to almost 425 °F.
3. Put pita bread on your greased pans and spoon peanut sauce (1/4) on every pita.
4. Sprinkle scallions (1/4) and chicken (1/4) on each pita and top each pizza with one slice of cheese.
5. Bake in your preheated oven for almost 12 minutes and leave it outside for nearly 2 minutes before cutting it with a pizza cutter.

17. Deep Dish Mexican Pizza Recipe

Preparation time: 20 minutes
Cooking time: 40 minutes
Servings: 4

Ingredients:

- 1 thick pizza crust
- Nonstick cooking spray
- 1/2 small onion -diced
- 1 teaspoon chili powder
- 1/2 teaspoon ground cumin
- 1/4 teaspoon ground cinnamon
- 15 ounces black beans -rinsed and drained
- 2 ounces diced green chilies
- 1 cup cornmeal
- 1 cup shredded monterey jack cheese
- 3/4 cup diced tomatoes
- 1/2 cup frozen whole kernel corn - thawed
- 1/2 green bell pepper -- diced
- 2 ounces sliced ripe black olives - drained
- 1/2 teaspoon olive oil

Directions:

1. Prepare pizza crust. Preheat oven to 500 °F. Spray 2-to 3-q uart saucepan with cooking spray. Place over medium heat.
2. Add onion, chili powder, cumin, cinnamon and 1 tablespoon water; stir.
3. Cover and cook 3 to 4 minutes or until onion is crisp-tender. Stirin beans and chilies.
4. Transfer 1/2 of the bean mixture to food processor or blender; process until almost smooth.
5. Spray 14-inch deep-dish pizza pan with nonstick cooking spray; sprinkle with cornmeal.
6. Press dough gently into bottom and up side of the pan. Cover with plastic wrap and let stand in warm place 15 to 20 minutes or until puffy. Bake 5 to 7 minutes or until dry and firm on top.
7. Spread pureed bean mixture over crust up to the thick edge.
8. Top with half the cheese, remaining bean mixture, tomatoes, corn, bell pepper, and olives. Top with remaining cheese.
9. Bake 10 to 12 minutes more or until crust is deep golden. Brush crust edges with olive oil. Cut into wedges.
10. Serve with salsa and sour cream.

18. Mayonnaise Burrito Pizzas Recipe

Preparation time: 20 minutes
Cooking time: 20 minutes
Servings: 4

Ingredients:

- 4 flour tortillas
- 8 ounces catsup
- 8 ounces freshly squeezed mayonnaise
- 8 ounces ez-cheese american
- 8 ounces ez-cheese cheddar

Directions:

1. Preheat oven to 350 °F.
2. Arrange the tortillas on cookie sheet.
3. Mix catsup and mayonnaise in bowl, divide into 4 portions, spread each portion onto each tortilla.
4. Top with cheese, half american and half cheddar.
5. Cook 15-20 minutes.
6. Serve.

19. Mexican Deep-Dish Pan Pizza Recipe

Preparation time: 20 minutes
Cooking time: 40 minutes
Servings: 4

Ingredients:

- 2 boxes (8.5 oz size) corn muffin mix
- 2 eggs
- 4 tablespoons melted butter
- 1 ½ cup milk
- 1 cup frozen corn kernels
- 1 cup extra-virgin olive oil or, vegetable oil, for drizzling

Toppings:

- 2 tablespoons extra-virgin or vegetable oil
- 1 pound ground beef
- 1 small onion, finely chopped
- 1 tablespoon chili powder
- 2 teaspoons ground cumin
- 2 teaspoons cayenne sauce
- 2 ½ cups shredded cheddar or jack cheese
- 1/2 red bell pepper, chopped
- 1 can (2 ¼ ounce sized) sliced jalapenos, drained
- 2 scallions, chopped
- 2 small vine ripe tomatoes, seeded and diced
- 2 tablespoons drained sliced green salad olives
- 2 tablespoons chopped cilantro leaves, optional garnis h
- 1 cup taco sauce

Directions:

1. Preheat oven to 400 °F.
2. Mix together the muffin mix with the eggs, melted butter, milk and frozen corn kernels. Lightly grease a large oven-safe nonstick skillet with oil and pour in the muffin mix. Place pan in oven and bake 12 to 15 minutes in center of the oven until light golden in color.
3. In another skillet over medium-high heat, brown the meat; add onions and spices and cook meat 5 minutes more.
4. Remove cornbread from oven and top with meat, cheese, and veggies. Add pan back to oven and cook 5 minutes more to melt cheese. Garnish with cilantro, optional.
5. Cut into 8 wedges and serve the deep dish pan pizza from the skillet. Pass taco sauce at the table to sprinkle on top.

20. BBQ Chicken Pizzas

Preparation time: 30 minutes
Cooking time: 5 minutes
Servings: 3

Ingredients:

- 2 packages (1/4 ounce each) active dry yeast
- 1 cup warm water (110° to 115°)
- 1/4 cup whole wheat flour
- 3 tablespoons olive oil
- 1 tablespoon honey
- 1 teaspoon salt
- 2 ¼ to 2 ¾ cups all-purpose flour

Toppings:

- 3/4 pound boneless skinless chicken breasts, cut into 1/2-inch pieces
- 1/2 medium red onion, thinly sliced and separated into rings
- 2 tablespoons olive oil, divided
- 3 garlic cloves, minced
- 1 cup barbecue sauce
- 2 cups shredded smoked Gouda cheese
- 1 cup shredded Asiago cheese
- 1/2 cup pickled pepper rings
- Minced fresh basil leaves, optional

Directions:

1. Dissolve the yeast in a big bowl with warm water.
2. Add oil, 1 ½ cups flour, whole wheat flour, salt, and honey. Mix until smooth. Stir in the rest of flour just until a soft dough is formed.
3. Put dough on a floured surface and knead for 6-8 minutes until it is smooth and like elastic. Put in a greased bowl, flip to coat top with grease. Cover and put it in a warm place and allow rise for about 1 hour or until doubled.
4. Punch down. Divide dough into four pieces on a slightly floured surface. Roll out every piece of dough into a 10-inch circle. Build up a small barrier around the edges.
5. Cover; let it sit for 10 minutes. In the meantime, put 1 tablespoon oil in a big frying pan, sauté onion and chicken until chicken is not pink. Now add garlic and cook for 1 minute. Mix in barbecue sauce; cook through.
6. Take away from heat and set it aside. Use cooking oil to moisten a paper towel; lightly grease the grill rack using long-handled tongs.
7. Use the remaining oil to brush on both sides of dough. Put the dough on the grill, cover, and grill on medium heat until crust is light brown, 1-2 minutes.
8. Take off the grill. On the grilled side of each of the pizzas layer with chicken mixture, pepper rings, and cheeses.
9. Put pizzas back on grill. Cover; cook until cheese melts and crust is light brown, 4-5 minutes. Halfway through cooking rotate the pizzas to make sure the crust browns evenly. If desired, sprinkle with basil.

21. BLT Pizza

Preparation time: 20 minutes
Cooking time: 15 minutes
Servings: 3

Ingredients:

- 4 slices bacon
- 1 (10-ounce) can of refrigerated pizza crust dough
- 1 teaspoon olive oil
- 2 cups mozzarella cheese, shredded
- 1 tomato, chopped
- 2 cups shredded iceberg lettuce
- 2 tablespoons mayonnaise, or to taste
- Salt and pepper to taste

Directions:

1. Heat the oven to 375 °F (190°C), or based on the instructions on the package of pizza dough.
2. Put bacon in a heavy skillet and fry over medium-high heat until brown but not crisp. Place on paper towels and drain.
3. Spread out the pizza dough over a cookie sheet, pan, or pizza stone. Use olive oil and brush the dough with it. Scatter the shredded mozzarella over the crust, and arrange the tomatoes over the cheese. Chop bacon, and scatter evenly over the pizza.
4. Place the pizza in the preheated oven and bake for 10 to 15 minutes, until cheese melts in the center and the crust turns golden. While baking the pizza, toss mayonnaise and shredded lettuce together, then lightly season with pepper and salt. Place the dressed lettuce on top of the finished pizza and serve right away.

22. Bacon Cheeseburger Pizza

Preparation time: 10 minutes
Cooking time: 10 minutes
Servings: 3

Ingredients:

- 1/2 pound ground beef
- 1 small onion, chopped
- 1 prebaked 12-inch pizza crust
- 1 can (8 ounces) pizza sauce
- 6 bacon strips, cooked and crumbled
- 20 dill pickle slices
- 2 cups shredded part-skim mozzarella cheese
- 2 cups shredded cheddar cheese
- 1 teaspoon of pizza or Italian seasoning

Directions:

1. In a big frying pan, cook onion and beef until the beef is not pink.
2. Drain excess grease and set the mixture aside.
3. In a 12-in. pan for pizza, put the crust. The pan should not be greased.
4. Spread pizza sauce on top.
5. Put bacon, beef mixture, pickles, and cheese on top.
6. Finally, sprinkle on the pizza seasoning.
7. Bake in a 450-degree oven until cheese melts, 8-10 minutes.

23. Bacon and Spinach Pizza

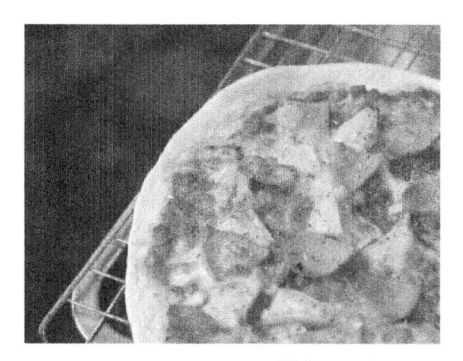

Preparation time: 10 minutes
Cooking time: 10 minutes
Servings: 3

Ingredients:

- 1 prebaked 12-inch pizza crust
- 1/3 cup pizza sauce
- 1 cup shaved Parmesan cheese
- 2 cups fresh baby spinach, thinly sliced
- 8 ready-to-serve fully cooked bacon strips, cut into 1-inch pieces

Directions:

1. Heat the oven to 450 °F.
2. Put crust on an ungreased baking sheet.
3. Smear with sauce; put bacon, spinach, and 1/2 cup cheese on top.
4. Scatter with the rest of the cheese.
5. Bake for 8 -10 minutes until the cheese melts.

24. Cold Vegetable Pizza

Preparation time: 10 minutes
Cooking time: 10 minutes
Servings: 3

Ingredients:

- 1 tube (4 ounces) refrigerated crescent rolls
- 1/4 cup mayonnaise
- 2 ounces cream cheese, softened
- 1/2 teaspoon dill weed
- 3/4 cup assorted chopped fresh vegetables (cucumber, radishes, red onion, green pepper, and/or mushrooms)
- 2 tablespoons sliced ripe olives
- 3 tablespoons finely shredded cheddar cheese
- 3 tablespoons finely shredded part-skim mozzarella cheese

Directions:

1. Unroll crescent rolls.
2. Put onto an ungreased baking sheet.
3. Flatten the dough to an 8x5-in. rectangle.
4. Seal perforations and seams.
5. Bake for 10 minutes until golden brown at 375 °F.
6. On a wire rack, cool.
7. Mix dill, cream cheese, and mayonnaise until blended in a small bowl. Spread on the crust.
8. Put veggies of your choice on top.
9. Sprinkle cheeses and olives.
10. Chill, covered, for at least 1 hour.
11. Cut to slices.
12. Keep leftovers in the fridge.

25. Colorful Crab Appetizer Pizza

Preparation time: 20 minutes
Cooking time: 10 minutes
Servings: 3

Ingredients:

- 1 tube (8 ounces) refrigerated crescent rolls
- 1 package (8 ounces) of cream cheese, softened
- 1½ cups coarsely chopped fresh spinach, divided
- 1 green onion, thinly sliced
- 1½ teaspoons minced fresh dill or 1/2 teaspoon dill weed
- 1 teaspoon grated lemon zest, divided
- 1/2 teaspoon lemon juice
- 1/8 teaspoon pepper
- 1 ¼ cups chopped imitation crabmeat
- 1/4 cup chopped ripe olives

Directions:

1. Unroll crescent roll dough.
2. Put on a 12-in. ungreased pizza pan.
3. Flatten dough—seal perforations and seams.
4. Bake for 8-10 minutes until lightly browned at 350 °F. Cool.
5. Beat cream cheese in a small bowl until smooth.
6. Mix pepper, lemon juice, 1/2 tsp. lemon zest, dill, onion, and 1 cup spinach. Spread on the crust.
7. Top with lemon peel, leftover spinach, olives, and crab.
8. Cut to bite-size squares.

26. Cornbread Pizza Wheels

Preparation time: 25 minutes
Cooking time: 15 minutes
Servings: 3

Ingredients:

- 1 pound ground beef
- 1 can (16 ounces) of kidney beans, rinsed and drained
- 1 can (8 ounces) of tomato sauce
- 4 teaspoons of chili powder
- 1 jar (4 ounces) of diced pimientos, drained
- 1 can (4 ounces) of chopped green chilies, drained
- 1 cup shredded cheddar cheese
- 2 tablespoons cornmeal
- 2 tubes (11½ ounces each) of refrigerated cornbread twists
- Shredded lettuce, sliced tomatoes, and sour cream

Directions:

1. Over medium heat, cook beef in a big skillet until no longer pink. Drain it, then put in chili powder, tomato sauce, and beans. Let it simmer until the liquid has evaporated without a cover. Move it away from heat and let it cool. Stir in cheese, chilies, and pimientos and set it aside.
2. Use cornmeal to sprinkle 2 greased 14 inches pizza pans. Make a 14 inches circle on each pan by patting cornbread dough. In the middle of the dough, cut a 7 inches "X" using a sharp knife. To form 8 pie-shaped wedges in the middle, cut another 7 inches "X."
3. Spoon the filling around the edge of the dough, then fold the points of the dough over the filling—tuck under the ring and seal by pinching it (the filling will be visible).
4. Now bake at about 400 °F until golden brown, about 15 to 20 minutes. Serve with sour cream, tomatoes, and lettuce.

27. Cranberry Camembert Pizza

Preparation time: 15 minutes
Cooking time: 20 minutes
Servings: 3

Ingredients:

- 8 ounces (1 round) Camembert cheese, cut into 1/2-inch cubes, rind removed
- (13.8 ounces) 1 tube refrigerated pizza crust
- 1/2 cup chopped pecans
- 3/4 cup whole-berry cranberry sauce

Directions:

1. On a lightly greased 12 inches pizza pan, unroll the crust.
2. Flatten the dough and slightly build up its edges.
3. Bake at 425 °F until light golden brown, about 10 to 12 minutes.
4. On top of the crust, sprinkle cheese then evenly spoon cranberry sauce over. Sprinkle with pecans.
5. Bake till cheese melted and crust is golden brown, about another 8 to 10 minutes. Before slicing, let it cool for 5 minutes.

28. Dartboard Pizza

Preparation time: 15 minutes
Cooking time: 15 minutes
Servings: 3

Ingredients:

- 1 tube (13.8 ounces) refrigerated pizza crust
- 1 can (8 ounces) pizza sauce
- 2 cups shredded part-skim mozzarella cheese
- 1 package (3 ½ ounces) sliced pepperoni
- 1 ½ cups shredded cheddar cheese
- 1 cup chopped green pepper

Directions:

1. On an ungreased 14 inches pizza pan, unroll the pizza crust. Flatten the dough and slightly build up its edges. Use a fork to prick the dough several times.
2. Bake at 425°F for 7 minutes, or until lightly browned. On a wire rack, let it cool. On top of the crust, spread the pizza sauce, then sprinkle mozzarella cheese.
3. In the middle of the pizza, put 1 pepperoni slice. Chop the leftover pepperoni. Around the outer edge of the pizza, sprinkle some chopped pepperoni, leaving half inch of crust. Sprinkle remaining pepperoni in a circle between the outer edge and the middle slice. In a spoke pattern, arrange alternately cheddar cheese and green pepper.
4. Bake at 425 °F until pizza is heated and cheese is melted about 12 minutes.

29. Dilly Veggie Pizza

Preparation time: 20 minutes
Cooking time: 10 minutes
Servings: 3

Ingredients:

- 1 tube (8 ounces) refrigerated crescent rolls
- 1 ½ cups vegetable dill dip
- 2 medium carrots, chopped
- 1 cup finely chopped fresh broccoli
- 1 cup chopped seeded tomatoes
- 4 green onions, sliced
- 1 can (2 ¼ ounces) sliced ripe olives, drained

Directions:

1. Unroll crescent dough into 1 long rectangle.
2. On the bottom of a 13x9-in. baking pan, press it in, then seal the seams. Bake for 10-12 minutes at 375 °F or until golden brown.
3. On a wire rack, completely cool.
4. Spread dip on the crust. Sprinkle olives, onions, tomatoes, broccoli, and carrots on.
5. Cut to squares. Refrigerate the leftovers.

30. Fantastic Artichoke Pizza

Preparation time: 10 minutes
Cooking time: 15 minutes
Servings: 3

Ingredients:

- 1 prebaked 12-inch pizza crust
- 1 can (14 ounces) water-packed artichoke hearts, rinsed, drained, and chopped
- 1 cup shredded Parmesan cheese, divided
- 1 cup shredded part-skim mozzarella cheese, divided
- 1 cup mayonnaise
- 6 garlic cloves, minced
- 1/2 cup sliced grape tomatoes

Directions:

1. On an ungreased 14-inch pizza pan, put crust.
2. Combine garlic, mayonnaise, 3/4 cup of each cheese, and artichokes in a small bowl. Spread it on top of the crust.
3. Put tomatoes on top.
4. Use the remaining cheese to sprinkle.
5. Bake until edges are lightly browned or for 15 to 20 minutes at 450 °F.

31. Festive Veggie Pizza

Preparation time: 15 minutes
Cooking time: 5 minutes
Servings: 3

Ingredients:

- Pastry for single-crust pie
- 2 packages (3 ounces each) of cream cheese, softened
- 1/4 cup crumbled blue cheese, optional
- 1/4 cup mayonnaise
- 1/4 teaspoon onion salt
- 1/4 teaspoon garlic salt
- 1 cup quartered cherry tomatoes
- 1/2 cup chopped broccoli
- 1/2 cup sliced fresh mushrooms
- 1/3 cup sliced ripe olives
- 1/4 cup chopped radishes
- 1 tablespoon minced fresh parsley, optional

Directions:

1. Roll out the pastry into an 11-inch circle on an ungreased baking sheet. Use a fork to prick it several times.
2. Bake until lightly browned at 425 °For for 8 minutes. On a wire rack, let it cool completely.
3. Meanwhile, beat blue cheese (optional), cream cheese, garlic salt, onion salt, and mayonnaise in a small bowl. Put the crust on a big serving plate, then spread the cream cheese mixture to within an inch of its edge. Cover and for at least 4 hours, let it chill.
4. If desired, put parsley, radishes, olives, mushrooms, broccoli, and tomatoes on top. Slice into serving-size pieces.

32. Mexican Pita Pizzas (Mexico) Recipe

Preparation time: 20 minutes
Cooking time: 20 minutes
Servings: 4

Ingredients:

- 4 pita breads
- 1 can black beans (15 oz) drained
- 1 can pico de gallo (11.5 oz) drained
- 1 cup cheese, cheddar shredded
- 1 cup cheese, Monterey jack shredded
- 2 cups lettuce shredded

Directions:

1. Heat oven to 375 °F.
2. Place pita bread on large baking sheet.
3. In medium bowl, combine beans, and pico deGallo. Spoon over pita bread. Sprinkle each with cheeses.
4. Bake 14 to 18 minutes or until heated through and cheese is melted.
5. Top with shredded lettuce.
6. Cut each into 6 wedges.
7. Serve with salsa, sour cream, guacamole, scallions and/or olives.

33. Freshly Baked Pesto Pizza

Preparation time: 10 minutes
Cooking time: 6 minutes
Servings: 4

Ingredients:

For Pesto:

- 1 cup extra virgin olive oil
- ½ cup almonds, blanched / toasted
- 2 tablespoons brined capers
- 3 garlic cloves
- 1 cup firmly packed fresh basil leaves
- ½ cup firmly packed fresh oregano leaves
- 4 ounces of crumbled feta cheese
- 1 ounce chopped kalamata olives
- 1 tablespoon fresh lemon juice
- 1 teaspoon black pepper
- ½ cup firmly packed fresh flat parsley leaves

For Pizza:

- 2 pieces 6-inch greek pita flatbreads
- ½ cup feta cheese
- 2 small tomatoes, chopped
- 8 pitted kalamata olives

Directions:

1. Take your food processor and add oil, capers, almonds, and garlic; process well. 2. Add herbs and process until nice and smooth.
2. Pour into a bowl and add feta, pepper, lemon juice, and olives; stir. Your pesto is now made.
3. Preheat oven to 350 °F.
4. Spread the pesto on top of each pita.
5. Top them with feta cheese, kalamata olives, and tomatoes.
6. Transfer the pita to a baking sheet and bake for about 6-8 minutes until the cheese melts nicely.

34. Cauliflower Pizza

Preparation time: 30 minutes
Cooking time: 30 minutes
Servings: 4

Ingredients:

- 1 medium cauliflower, trimmed and broken into small florets
- 2 tablespoons extra-virgin olive oil, divided
- ¼ teaspoon salt
- 1 large lemon
- 6 oil-packed sun-dried tomatoes, drained and coarsely chopped
- 1/3 cup black olives, pitted and sliced
- 1 large egg, slightly beaten
- 1 cup shredded, part-skim mozzarella cheese
- ½ teaspoon dried oregano
- 2 tablespoons freshly ground pepper
- ¼ cup fresh basil, slivered

Directions:

1. Preheat oven to 450 °F.
2. Line a pizza pan with parchment paper.
3. In a food processor, pulse cauliflower until it is in rice-size chunks.
4. Place cauliflower in a large nonstick pan and cook over medium heat.
5. Add 1 tablespoon of oil and salt.
6. Cook the cauliflower for about 8-10 minutes until they are soft.
7. Put the mixture in a bowl and set it aside to cool for ten min. Take a sharp knife and skin the white pith from your lemon.
8. Work all the way around the segments from the membranes, allowing the segments to fall into a bowl.
9. Remove the seeds and drain the juice.
10. Add tomatoes and olives to the lemon segments; toss well to combine.
11. Add egg, oregano, and cheese to the cooled cauliflower; stir to combine everything well.
12. Spread the cauliflower mixture into a 10-inch round pizza.
13. Drizzle 1 teaspoon of olive oil all over.
14. Bake the pizza for about 10-14 minutes.
15. Remove and scatter the lemon and olive mixture on top.
16. Season with pepper and bake for another 8-14 minutes until it is nicely browned all over.
17. Scatter some basil on top.
18. Slice the pizza into wedges and enjoy!

35. Neapolitan Pizza

Preparation time: 15 minutes + inactive time
Cooking time: 8 minutes
Servings: 2 pizzas

Ingredients:

For the Dough:

- 2 cups bread flour
- 2 teaspoons fine salt
- 1 teaspoon instant yeast
- 1¼ cups water

For the Toppings:

- 1 cup san Marzano crushed tomatoes
- 1 cup mozzarella, torn into pieces
- Basil, as desired

Directions:

1. To make the dough, combine flour, salt, and yeast in a bowl.
2. Make a well in the center. Pour in the water and start stirring with a fork, gradually adding flour into the water.
3. Once it is incorporated, transfer the dough onto a flour-dusted kitchen surface.
4. Knead the dough for 10 minutes. Place the dough in a bowl that has been greased gently and cover it with clingfilm.
5. Allow the dough to rise for 12 hours.
6. Shape the dough into two equal balls. Place the dough balls into separate containers, in the refrigerator, and allow them to rise for 2 days more.
7. Remove the dough from the refrigerator 2 hours before baking.
8. Stretch the dough to 13 ½ inches in diameter.
9. Preheat oven to 400 °F.
10. Place the pizza dough on the pizza stone. Top with tomato sauce, basil, and mozzarella.
11. Bake for 8 minutes.
12. Serve warm.

36. Sicilian Pizza

Preparation time: 15 minutes + rising time
Cooking time: 20 minutes
Servings: 6-8

Ingredients:

For the Dough:

- 4 cups all-purpose flour
- 2 teaspoons sea salt
- 2 teaspoons fine sugar
- 1 teaspoon instant yeast
- 1¾ cups lukewarm water
- ¼ cup olive oil

For the Toppings:

- 1 tablespoon olive oil
- 1 onion, diced
- 2 cloves garlic, minced
- 2 cups crushed san Marzano tomatoes
- 2 teaspoons dried oregano
- 12oz. Mozzarella, torn into pieces

Directions:

1. Combine flour, salt, sugar, and yeast in a bowl.
2. Make a well in the center.
3. Pour in water and olive oil.
4. Stir gently with your hands and continue stirring until the dough comes together.
5. Transfer the dough to the flour-dusted surface.
6. Knead the dough for approx. 10 minutes until smooth. Transfer the dough to the oiled bowl and allow it to rest overnight.
7. Stretch the dough into an 11-inch baking sheet and cover it with plastic foil. Allow rising for an additional 2 hours. Preheat oven to 450 °F.
8. In the meantime, make the sauce; heat olive oil in a skillet. Add onion and cook for 6 minutes.
9. Add garlic and cook 1 minute. Add tomatoes and oregano.
10. Simmer for 5 minutes.
11. Take the sauce off the heat and put it in a cold place. Spread the cooled sauce over the dough. Top with mozzarella.

12. Bake the pizza in the heated oven for 20 minutes.

13. Serve warm.

37. Garlic Pizza with Mozzarella

Preparation time: 1 hour
Cooking time: 15 minutes
Servings: 4

Ingredients:

For the Dough:

- 1 cup all-purpose flour
- 1 cup lukewarm water
- 1 egg yolk
- ½ teaspoon salt

For the Toppings:

- 2 cups mozzarella
- 3 garlic cloves, sliced
- 2 tablespoons sour cream
- 2 tablespoons olive oil
- Thyme

Directions:

1. In a mixing basin, sift together the flour and salt.
2. Add butter and egg yolk and mix.
3. Pour in warm water and knead the dough tightly.
4. Put the dough on the table and knead well. Cover with film and set aside for 30 minutes. 5. The dough will become much softer in half an hour.
5. Roll the dough into a thin circle and transfer it to a baking tray covered with parchment paper (grease the paper).
6. Lubricate the dough with sour cream.
7. Spread out the garlic and pieces of mozzarella. Add salt and sprinkle with thyme.
8. Bake for 15 minutes. Eat right away!

38. Four-Cheese Pizza

Preparation time: 20 minutes
Cooking time: 10 minutes
Servings: 4

Ingredients:

- 18 oz. Pizza dough
- ½ cup tomato puree
- 1 cup mozzarella cheese, grated, divided
- ½ cup Emmental cheese, grated
- ¼ cup blue cheese, crumbled
- 1 tablespoon parmesan cheese, grated
- ¼ cup münster cheese
- 1 tablespoon olive oil

Directions:

1. Prepare the dough for the pizza. Roll out, grease with tomato sauce, and sprinkle with a ¾ cup of mozzarella Cheese.
2. Distribute emmental, crumbled blue cheese, and münster.
3. Then put the remaining mozzarella cheese on top and sprinkle it with parmesan cheese.
4. Preheat oven and bake pizza for 8-10 minutes.

39. Delicate Seafood Pizza

Preparation time: 1 hour
Cooking time: 20 minutes
Servings: 2

Ingredients:

For the Dough:

- 1 cup all-purpose flour
- ½ cup wheat flour, whole-grain
- ½ cup warm water
- ½ teaspoon yeast
- 1 teaspoon of sea salt
- 1 tablespoon sugar
- 1½ tablespoons olive oil

For the Toppings:

- 2 cups shrimp
- 5 cherry tomatoes
- 2 big tomatoes
- 1 cup parmesan cheese, grated
- 1 teaspoon oregano
- 1 teaspoon of basil
- 1 teaspoon olive oil

Directions:

1. First, make a dough—mix yeast with water and sugar. Leave in a warm place for 10 minutes until the foam appears.
2. Strain both kinds of flour and salt in a separate bowl.
3. Knead the dough for at least 5 minutes, pouring in the whole-grain flour gradually. The dough should become smooth and elastic and slightly stick to your hands.
4. Tuck it in a warm location for 40 minutes with a towel over it. It will double in size.
5. For the sauce, cut the big tomatoes, remove the seeds, and chop. Blend together with olive oil, dried herbs, and salt.
6. Roll the dough into a circle with a thickness of 1/5 in., spread the sauce over the base, and put it in a preheated 360 °F oven for 5-7 minutes.
7. Defrost the shrimp (I just pour boiling water over them). Remove the base from the oven and put the shrimp, cheese, cherry tomatoes in half. Sprinkle with salt and pink pepper. Sprinkle with olive oil.
8. Put in the oven for another 10-15 minutes. Top with basil. Bon appetit!

40. Pizza Marinara

Preparation time: 2 hours
Cooking time: 20 minutes
Servings: 4

Ingredients:

For the Dough:

- 1 cup all-purpose flour
- ¾ cup water
- 1 teaspoon yeast
- 1 tablespoon olive oil

For the Toppings:

- 2 cups shrimp
- 2 cups mussels
- 2 tablespoons parmesan cheese, grated
- 2 tomatoes
- basil, oregano, to taste
- ground black pepper, to taste
- salt, to taste
- 1 tablespoon olive oil

Directions:

1. Combine the sifted flour with dry yeast, salt, oil, and warm water.
2. Stir well and knead the dough.
3. Cover the dough with a kitchen towel for 40 minutes and put it in a warm place.
4. Then roll the dough into a thin layer, put it on the oiled baking sheet, and form the sides.
5. Boil shrimp and mussels in boiling salted water. Then cool and cut into pieces.
6. Blanche the tomatoes in boiling water, peel them, and cut them into small slices. Fry tomatoes for 3 minutes in hot oil. Sprinkle with basil, mix, remove from heat, and cool.
7. Put the tomato paste on the dough.
8. Then top with the seafood, evenly distributed. Sprinkle with pepper, oregano, and grated cheese.
9. Bake in the oven at 400 °F for half an hour.
10. Then get it out of the oven, put it on a dish, cut it into small pieces, and serve.

41. Tuna Pizza

Preparation time: 20 minutes
Cooking time: 20 minutes
Servings: 4

Ingredients:

For the Dough:

- 1¼ cups all-purpose flour
- ½ cup milk
- 2 tablespoons butter
- 1 tablespoon yeast
- 2 teaspoons sugar
- 2 whole eggs

For the Toppings:

- 2 cups smoked ham
- 3 tomatoes
- 1 can of tuna in oil
- 2 bell peppers
- 2 tablespoons olives
- 2 tablespoons olive oil
- 2 tablespoon mayonnaise
- Pinch of salt
- Ground black pepper, to taste
- Parsley greens

Directions:

1. Knead the yeast dough, roll it out and lay it on the baking sheet, slightly bending the edges.
2. Grind the fish and evenly place it on the dough.
3. Place the tomatoes cut into small pieces on top of the dough.
4. Peel the sweet pepper from the seeds and cut them into half rings. Add to the pizza.
5. Decorate with olives and chopped parsley.
6. Pour oil and grease with mayonnaise.
7. Put the pizza in a hot oven for 20 minutes.

42. Pizza Di Mare (With Seafood)

Preparation time: 1 hour
Cooking time: 25 minutes
Servings: 2

Ingredients:

For the Dough:

- ¾ cup all-purpose flour
- ½ cup wheat flour, whole-grain
- 1 whole egg
- ½ cup warm water
- ½ teaspoon yeast
- ½ teaspoon of sea salt
- 1 teaspoon sugar
- 3 tablespoons olive oil

For the Toppings:

- 4 tablespoons tomato sauce with olives
- 1 cup parmesan cheese, grated
- fresh basil
- 1 teaspoon olive oil
- 2 cups seafood cocktail (shrimp, mussels, squid, octopus)

Directions:

1. Mix the flour, yeast, salt, and sugar in a bowl. Beat the egg with water and olive oil in a bowl with a fork. Mix the dry ingredients with liquid and knead the elastic dough. Leave for 1 hour until the dough doubles in size.
2. Roll the dough into a thin layer, and put it on a baking tray or a special pizza dish.
3. Spread the dough with the tomato paste.
4. Top with the basil leaves and sprinkle with grated cheese.
5. Layout seafood evenly. Put the pizza in a preheated oven for 20-25 minutes.
6. Before serving, sprinkle with olive oil infused with fragrant herbs. Bon appetit!

43. Vegetarian Pizza

Preparation time: 30 minutes
Cooking time: 25 minutes
Servings: 4

Ingredients:

For the Dough:

- 1 cup all-purpose flour
- 1 whole egg
- ½ cup milk
- 3 tablespoons olive oil
- 1 teaspoon yeast
- ½ teaspoon of sea salt

For the Toppings:

- 8 tomatoes
- 2 cups champignon mushrooms, sliced
- 1 cup cheddar cheese, grated
- 1 onion raw
- 6 tablespoons olive oil
- ½ teaspoon of sea salt
- ground black pepper
- greens

Directions:

1. Mix all the ingredients for the dough. Cover it with a cloth and keep it in a warm area to rise.
2. Cut and sauté the onions.
3. Grind tomatoes and greens.
4. Roll out the finished dough into a 1 cm thick flat cake and place it on a greased baking sheet.
5. Put the mushrooms on top of the dough and season with salt and pepper.
6. Decorate the pizza with fried onion rings and tomato slices.
7. Sprinkle the pizza with grated cheese and add shredded greens. Sprinkle with olive oil.
8. Bake at a temperature of 360-390 °F for approximately 25 minutes.

44. Bell Pepper Pizza

Preparation time: 20 minutes
Cooking time: 10 minutes
Servings: 4

Ingredients:

For the Dough:

- 1 cup all-purpose flour
- ½ cup warm water
- 1 tablespoon olive oil
- 1 teaspoon yeast
- ½ teaspoon of sea salt
- ½ teaspoon sugar

For the Toppings:

- 1 tomato
- 3 bell peppers in different colors
- 1 cup parmesan cheese, grated
- 1 onion
- 2 garlic cloves
- 1 teaspoon salt
- 1 teaspoon ground red pepper
- Oregano

Directions:

1. Mix ingredients for the dough, knead, roll it out, and put it on a greased baking sheet.
2. Peel the onion, garlic, and tomato and cut them into small pieces.
3. Sauté the onions and garlic in half the oil until golden. Add salt, pepper, and tomato. Stir and simmer for 5 minutes, then cool.
4. Remove the stalk and seeds from the peppers and cut them into half rings.
5. Spread the tomato paste evenly on the oiled base.
6. Sprinkle half the cheese, spread the pepper halves, and sprinkle with the remaining cheese, and oregano.
7. Put the baking sheet in an oven preheated to 390 °F and bake for 10 minutes.

45. Pan Pizza Crust

Preparation time: 20 minutes
Cooking time: 12 to 15 minutes
Servings: 4

Ingredients:

- 2 ½ cups unbleached all-purpose flour
- 2 tsp salt
- ½ tsp instant dry yeast
- 1 cup, plus 3 tbsp water
- 2 tsp olive oil

For the Rectangular Crust:

- 3 ½ cups unbleached all-purpose flour
- 2 ¾ tsp salt
- 3/4 tsp instant dry yeast
- 1 2/3 cups water
- 3 tbsp olive oil

Directions:

1. Grease two pizza pans or cast-iron skillets once the dough is ready.
2. Spread oil on your hands and punch the dough to deflate.
3. Divide into two equal halves and roll each into a ball. As required, lubricate your hands.
4. Place one portion on a greased pizza pan and shape by pushing down and towards the pan's edges. Repeat with the remaining dough.
5. Cover the formed dough with plastic wrap and spread it with oil.
6. Allow for 1 hour before pushing towards the sides again.
7. Allow for another hour of relaxation. Preheat the oven to 550 °F at the same time.
8. Spread chosen sauce and garnishes over each dough circle.
9. Cook till golden brown (about 12-15 minutes).
10. If necessary, remove from pan and serve immediately.

46. Pizza Crust Without Yeast

Preparation time: 20 minutes
Cooking time: 35 minutes
Servings: 8

Ingredients:

- 1 ⅓ cups flour
- 1 tsp. baking powder
- Dash of salt
- 2 minced garlic cloves
- 1 tsp. oregano
- ½ cup milk
- 1 tbsp. olive oil

Directions:

1. Combine the flour, baking powder, salt, garlic, and oregano in a bowl.
2. Add the milk and olive oil and combine well.
3. Flour a flat surface, then proceed to knead the dough 12 times.
4. Create a ball.
5. Cover the ball with a moist towel and let it rest for 10 minutes.
6. Use a rolling pin to create a 12-inch crust.
7. Place the crust on a baking sheet or pizza stone.
8. Bake for 10 minutes at 400 °F.
9. Put toppings of your choice and bake for another 15 minutes.

47. Goat Pizza

Preparation time: 10 minutes
Cooking time: 15 minutes
Servings: 4

Ingredients:

- 1 medium pizza base
- 2 cups mozzarella cheese, grated
- 2 cups stir-fried goat chunks
- 2 tbsp. pizza sauce
- Dried oregano and chili flakes for seasoning
- Salt and pepper to taste

Directions:

1. Preheat the oven to 350 ºF.
2. Spread a pizza sauce over the pizza base and sprinkle mozzarella over each half. Add goat's chunks to the pizza in an even layer. Add salt and pepper.
3. Now, place the pizza over the oven's grill.
4. Bake for 15 minutes or until cheese melts completely and turns golden brown.
5. Once ready, take the pizza from the oven.
6. Season with dried oregano and chili flakes.
7. Then, transfer the pizza to a serving platter and make 6 equal slices with the help of a pizza cutter.
8. Serve hot!

48. Yeast-Free Pizza Dough

Preparation time: 15 minutes
Cooking time: 15 minutes
Servings: 1 pizza dough

Ingredients:

- 2 cups all-purpose flour
- 2½ teaspoons baking soda, aluminum-free
- ¾ cup water
- ¾ teaspoon fine salt
- ¾ tablespoon olive oil

Directions:

1. Combine baking soda, flour, and salt in a large bowl.
2. In a separate, small bowl, combine water and olive oil.
3. Fold the liquid ingredients into the dry ones and start stirring with a fork until the dough comes together.
4. Transfer the dough onto a flour-dusted surface and knead until smooth.
5. Pulling and stretching the pizza dough with your hands and fingers, place it on a baking sheet that has been lightly oiled.
6. Top with the desired topping.
7. Bake the pizza in the preheated oven at 400 °F for 15 minutes.
8. Serve pizza warm.

49. Classic Tomato Sauce

Preparation time: 5 minutes
Cooking time: 15 minutes
Servings: approximately 4 cups

Ingredients:

- 4 garlic cloves, peeled
- 15-oz. Can diced tomatoes, with juices
- 1 tablespoon balsamic vinegar
- 8 leaves basil
- 2 tablespoons olive oil
- 1 teaspoon brown sugar
- ¾ teaspoon salt

Directions:

1. Press the garlic through the garlic press and transfer it into a food processor.
2. In the food processor, combine the remaining ingredients.
3. Process the ingredients until they are smooth and chunk-free.
4. Store the pizza sauce in a jar or use it immediately.

Note: You can cook this sauce as well and make it thicker. If you want a tomato sauce with longer-shelf life, simmer the sauce for 20 minutes. But, if you want a sauce with a brilliantly refreshing aroma, we suggest you make this sauce as it is – without any cooking involved.

50. Basil Garlic Sauce

Preparation time: 5 minutes
Cooking time: 15 minutes
Servings: 1 cup

Ingredients:

- 1 cup packed basil
- 3 cloves garlic, minced
- ¼ cup olive oil
- ¼ cup grated parmesan cheese
- ¼ teaspoon salt
- Pepper, to taste

Directions:

1. Combine basil and garlic in a food blender.
2. Blend on high until smooth.
3. Drizzle in the olive oil and blend for 1 minute.
4. Stir in the parmesan cheese and seasonings.
5. You can use the sauce immediately or store it in the fridge for a week.

51. Pumpkin Pizza Sauce

Preparation time: 10 minutes
Cooking time: 40 minutes
Servings: 3 cups

Ingredients:

- 1 Hokkaido pumpkin
- 4 tablespoons olive oil, divided
- 1 tablespoon honey
- 1 pinch cinnamon
- 1 pinch nutmeg
- 2 baking apples
- Salt, to taste
- 2 sage sprigs, leaves only

Directions:

1. Preheat oven to 400 °F.
2. Take out the seeds and inner threads from the pumpkin by cutting it in half.
3. Brush the pumpkin with half the olive oil and place it onto the roasting sheet. Sprinkle with sage leaves.
4. Place the apples next to the pumpkin.
5. Roast for 40 minutes or until the pumpkin is soft.
6. Remove the pumpkin and apples from the oven. Place aside to cool down.
7. Scrape the flesh and place it in a large bowl.
8. Cut the apple and remove the apple flesh—place in a bowl with the pumpkin.
9. Stir in the remaining olive oil, honey, cinnamon, and nutmeg.
10. Continue to stir until smooth.
11. Use the sauce immediately or store it for 4 days in a refrigerator.

52. White Pizza Sauce

Preparation time: 5 minutes
Cooking time: 10 minutes
Servings: 2½ cups

Ingredients:

- 4 tablespoons butter
- 2 shallots, diced
- 4 cloves garlic, minced
- 1 tablespoon flour
- 2 cups heavy cream, room temperature
- ½ teaspoon fresh basil
- Salt, to taste

Directions:

1. Heat butter in a saucepot over medium-high heat.
2. Add shallots and cook for 6 minutes.
3. Add minced garlic and cook until very fragrant. At this stage, watch your garlic so it does not burn.
4. Add the flour and cook, stirring until the flour has changed color; it should be slightly yellowish. Do not burn your flour; otherwise, your sauce will have a rather repulsive flavor.
5. Pour in heavy cream and whisk vigorously to remove any lumps.
6. Simmer the heavy cream for a few minutes or until thickened. Stir in basil and remove from heat.
7. Allow your sauce to cool down. Use immediately.

53. Pizza Napolitano

Preparation time: 3 hours
Cooking time: 20 minutes
Servings: 4

Ingredients:

For the Dough:

- 1 cup all-purpose flour
- ½ cup warm water
- 1 tablespoon olive oil
- 1 teaspoon yeast
- ½ teaspoon sugar

For the Toppings:

- 2 cups smoked ham
- 1 cup cheese
- 4 tomatoes
- 2 parsley roots
- 1 teaspoon green onion, to taste
- 1 teaspoon salt, to taste
- 1 teaspoon ground black pepper, to taste

Directions:

1. Knead the dough, let rise, once again mix well, and roll into a layer 5 mm thick.
2. Lay the base of the pizza on a greased baking sheet.
3. Prepare the sour cream sauce. Grate cheese on a large grater, mix with sour cream, salt, and pepper, and add finely chopped green onions.
4. Oil the pizza sauce.
5. Cut the ham into circles, and cut the tomatoes into rings.
6. Boil the root of parsley and finely chop.
7. Spread out the filling on the oiled base.
8. Bake pizza in the oven for 20 minutes.

54. Pizza Regina

Preparation time: 20 minutes
Cooking time: 25 minutes
Servings: 4

Ingredients:

For the Dough:

- 2½ cups all-purpose flour
- 1½ cups warm water
- 1 tablespoon butter
- 1 tablespoon yeast
- 1 tablespoon of sea salt
- 1 teaspoon sugar

For the Toppings:

- 6 tomatoes
- 6 big black olives, ripe, canned
- 2 cups ham
- 2 cups mozzarella cheese
- 2 cups champignon mushrooms
- 3 tablespoons olive oil
- ¼ onion

For the Italian Sauce:

- 4 tomatoes
- 1 onion
- 5 garlic cloves
- 1 tablespoon oregano
- 2 tablespoons ketchup
- 3 tablespoons olive oil
- 1 tablespoon sugar
- Ground black pepper
- Salt

Directions:

1. Mix water and yeast in a mixer for 5 minutes.
2. Add flour, salt, and sugar to the mixture. Mix until smooth.
3. Cover the dough with a towel and put it in a warm place for 1½ hours.
4. Then move the dough to the refrigerator and leave it there for 1 hour.
5. Prepare the Italian sauce. Chop the onion and then sauté with garlic in olive oil until the onions are transparent.
6. Add oregano, ketchup, sugar, salt, and pepper. Cook on medium heat until the sauce is evaporated by a third (about half an hour).
7. Add the tomatoes, peeled and chopped.
8. Continue to simmer until the sauce thickens.
9. Then brown the ham on medium heat.
10. Fry the onion rings in the remaining butter after frying the ham.
11. Form the base, greasing your hands with olive oil. The cake should turn out to be thin but not transparent.
12. Use a fork to make several holes in the base.
13. Spread the base with olive oil first, then Italian sauce.
14. Put the fried onions and chopped mushrooms on top of that.
15. Then arrange the slices of fried ham and sliced tomatoes.
16. Sprinkle with cheese, grated on a large grater. Add olives if desired.
17. Bake at 430 °F for about 20 minutes.

55. Pizza Capriccio

Preparation time: 30 minutes
Cooking time: 15 minutes
Servings: 4

Ingredients:

- 10 oz. Pizza dough
- 1 cup champignon mushrooms, sliced
- 1 onion
- 6 cherry tomatoes, halved
- ½ cup ricotta cheese
- ½ cup parmesan cheese, grated
- ¼ cup jumbo olives
- 1 cup pork sausage, sliced
- ½ cup smoked salmon
- 2 tablespoons olive oil
- Ground black pepper
- Salt
- Dill greens, chopped

Directions:

1. Cut the onion into rings.
2. Cut the olives in circles.
3. Lubricate the dough with half of the olive oil and roll it into a round cake with a diameter of 12 in.
4. Top with toppings: mushrooms, half of the onions, sausage, ricotta cheese, olives, salmon with the remaining onions, and tomatoes.
5. Add salt and pepper, and sprinkle the pizza with dill and parmesan cheese.
6. Place the prepared pizza on a greased baking sheet, and put it in an oven preheated to 400 °F. Bake for 15 minutes.

56. Pepperoni Pizza

Preparation time: 2½ hours
Cooking time: 20 minutes
Servings: 4

Ingredients:

For the Dough:

- 2 cups all-purpose flour
- 1 cup warm water
- 1 tablespoon butter, melted
- 1½ teaspoons yeast
- 1 whole egg, lightly beaten
- 1 tablespoon sugar

For the Toppings:

- 1 tomato, sliced
- 3 bell peppers, chopped
- 1 cup pepperoni, sliced
- 1 cup champignon mushrooms, chopped
- 1 cup parmesan cheese, grated
- 1 hot chili pepper, chopped
- 4 tablespoons tomato sauce
- 3 tablespoons mayonnaise
- Basil

Directions:

1. Place the yeast in a glass of warm water, and add sugar and flour. Stir.
2. Add an egg, salt, and butter to the dough, and knead.
3. Leave the dough in a warm place for 2 hours. The finished dough should be soft.
4. Fry mushrooms for 3-4 minutes.
5. Place the cake of the dough on a dry baking sheet, sprinkled with flour, and mash/spread it to a thickness of 5 mm.
6. Spread the dough with tomato sauce, and then cover it with pepperoni, mushrooms, peppers, and tomatoes.
7. Then spread the pizza with mayonnaise and sprinkle with cheese and chili peppers.
8. Bake pizza for 20 minutes at 430 °F.

57. Black Olives Salami Pizza

Preparation time: 30 minutes
Cooking time: 25 minutes
Servings: 4

Ingredients

For the Dough:

- 2 cups all-purpose flour
- 2 tablespoons sugar
- 1 whole egg
- ¾ cup warm water
- ½ cup butter
- 1 teaspoon yeast
- ½ teaspoon salt

For the Toppings:

- 2 tomatoes
- 1 bell pepper
- 1 can of black olives
- 1½ cups sliced cooked salami, sliced
- 3 tablespoons tomato sauce
- 2 cups grated cheese
- 1 teaspoon basil
- 1 teaspoon oregano

Directions:

1. Prepare the dough by combining the above-listed ingredients. Don't add oil to it.
2. Cool the dough in the refrigerator to 70 °F.
3. Then roll the dough into a layer 1.5 cm thick.
4. Cover the top half of the layer with soft butter and fold it in half. Flour.
5. Roll it out again.
6. Put the dough on a baking tray, oiled with butter.
7. Spread the dough with tomato sauce.
8. Chop up the above-listed ingredients for the topping.
9. Put all the ingredients on top of the oiled dough.
10. Sprinkle with cheese, oregano, and basil.
11. Bake in the oven at 340-370 °F for approximately 25 minutes.

58. Yummy Veggie Pizza

Preparation time: 20 minutes
Cooking time: 12 minutes
Servings: 4

Ingredients:

- 2 packages of crescent dinner rolls
- ½ cup dry ranch dressing mix
- 1 cup broccoli, chopped
- 1 cup cheddar cheese, shredded
- ¼ cup bell pepper
- ½ cup mayonnaise
- 1/3 cup black olives
- 1 cup cream cheese
- 1/3 cup cauliflower florets, chopped
- ½ cup carrots, chopped

Directions

1. Preheat oven to 370 °F.
2. Grease a baking sheet with oil.
3. Arrange crescent rolls into rectangles while pressing the seams together.
4. Place them on the baking sheet.
5. Bake in the oven for 12 minutes until golden brown.
6. Meanwhile, take a separate bowl and combine cream cheese, mayonnaise, and dressing mix.
7. Spread this mixture over the cooled crust evenly.
8. Top the crust with broccoli, cauliflower, olives, bell pepper, and carrots.
9. Sprinkle with cheese. Slice and serve.

59. Fresh Vegetable Pizza

Preparation time: 20 minutes
Cooking time: 15 minutes
Servings: 4

Ingredients:

- 2 packages of crescent dinner rolls
- 1/6 teaspoon pepper
- 2 cups mushrooms, chopped
- ½ cup green bell pepper, chopped
- ½ cup green onions
- 1 cup seeded tomatoes
- 1 cup broccoli florets
- 10 ounces sour cream
- 2 tablespoons horseradish
- Pinch of salt

Directions:

1. First, preheat the oven to 355 °F.
2. Spread the dough onto a flat surface to form a round shape.
3. Place it in a large baking pan.
4. Press into the bottom and up sides to form the crust.
5. Bake for 15 minutes until golden brown.
6. Let it cool.
7. Mix thoroughly in a bowl and combine sour cream, horseradish, salt, and pepper.
8. Spread this mixture all over the crust.
9. Top with all the remaining listed ingredients. Cut into slices and serve.

60. Vegan Pizza

Preparation time: 20 minutes
Cooking time: 2 hours
Servings: 4

Ingredients:

- 1 cup cashews, dried
- 2 teaspoons lemon juice
- 2 garlic cloves
- 1 teaspoon herbs de Provence spice blend
- 2 tablespoons water
- 2 tablespoons of almond meal
- Sea salt, to taste

For Crust:

- 1 red bell pepper
- ½ cup sunflower seeds
- 1 teaspoon black pepper, to taste
- Pinch of salt
- For the Toppings: 2 cups cauliflower florets, chopped
- ½ cup baby spinach
- 1 cup black olives
- ½ teaspoon ginger garlic paste
- ingredients for sauce
- 1 cup chopped tomatoes
- ½ cup sun-dried tomatoes
- 2 teaspoons lemon juice
- 4 dates
- 1 teaspoon fresh basil
- Salt and black pepper, to taste

Directions:

1. Take a blender and blend all the vegan cheese ingredients to make a paste.
2. Wrap it in cheesecloth and place it in a bowl.
3. Leave it for 2 days to let it dry.
4. Now, make a crust for pizza. For that, place all the crust ingredients in a blender and then pulse for a few seconds to combine it into a wet dough.
5. Spread this wet dough onto parchment paper and dehydrate it in the microwave for 2 hours.
6. You can use a dehydrator as well.
7. Blend all the sauce ingredients in a blender and set aside.
8. Now assemble the pizza by spreading the sauce on the crust and covering it with toppings and cheese.
9. Serve and enjoy.

61. Cheese Pizza Calzone

Preparation time: 30 minutes
Cooking time: 10 minutes
Servings: 4

Ingredients:

- 10 oz. Pizza dough
- 1 cup cheddar cheese
- 1 cup gouda cheese, grated
- 1 cup ricotta cheese
- 1 cup parmesan cheese, grated
- 1 whole egg
- 1 tablespoon extra-virgin olive oil
- Sea salt, to taste
- White ground pepper, to taste
- Parsley, dill, to taste

Directions:

1. Chop the greens of dill and parsley and mix with grated cheese except for parmesan.
2. Sprinkle with salt and pepper.
3. Roll out two thin cakes of pizza dough with a diameter of 25 cm and grease them with oil.
4. Layout the filling on one cake, and then cover it with the other. Protect the edges.
5. Brush the top with a beaten egg and sprinkle with the remaining greens and parmesan cheese.
6. Put the pizza on a greased baking sheet.
7. Place in an oven preheated to 390 °F and bake for 10 minutes.

62. Buttermilk Biscuit Dough

Preparation time: 10 minutes
Cooking time: 35 minutes
Servings: 12

Ingredients:

- All-purpose flour: 2 cups
- Butter (unsalted): 7 tbsp. (put in the freezer and cut thin slices)
- Cold buttermilk: ¾ cup
- Baking powder: 2 tsp.
- Buttermilk: 2 tbsp. (only for brushing)
- Salt: 1 tsp.
- Baking soda: ¼ tsp.

Directions:

1. Preheat your oven to almost 425 °F. One baking sheet should be lined with baking mat or parchment paper.
2. Whisk baking soda, salt, baking powder, and flour in one large bowl. Cut frozen butter into flour, blend with one pastry blender, and mix it well for almost 5 minutes to make a mixture similar to coarse crumbs.
3. Make one well in the middle of the flour and butter mixture, pour buttermilk (3/4 cup), and stir well to combine. Turn dough on your floured surface and pat together to make a rectangle.
4. Fold rectangles in thirds and roll the dough in half. Gather all crumbs and make them flat in a rectangle. Replicate this procedure twice, and fold and press this dough almost three times.
5. Roll dough on your floured surface to make a ½-inch thick disk and cut out desired rounds. You can transfer these to your baking sheet, top them with desired toppings, and brush them with buttermilk (2 tbsp.). Bake in your preheated oven for almost 15 minutes.

63. Bubble Pizza with Beef

Preparation time: 10 minutes
Cooking time: 40 minutes
Servings: 8

Ingredients:

- Ground beef: 1 pound
- Black olives (sliced): 10 ounces
- Pepperoni sausage (sliced): ¼ pound
- Sliced mushrooms: 4.5 ounce
- Mozzarella cheese (shredded): 1 ½ cups
- Pizza sauce: 14 ounces
- Cheddar cheese (shredded): 1 cup
- Buttermilk dough: 12 ounces (see next recipe)
- Sliced onions (rings): 1/2

Directions:

1. Preheat your oven to almost 400 °F. Grease one baking dish (9x13-inch).
2. Cook ground beef in a deep skillet over medium flame to make it equally brown and mix in pepperoni; cook it well until browned. Drain extra fat and add pizza sauce to this mixture. Mix well and turn off the heat.
3. Cut biscuit dough into quarters and put them in the bottom of your baking dish. Spread the cooked meat mixture equally over the biscuits and sprinkle with mushrooms, olives, and onion.
4. Bake it without cover in your preheated oven for almost 20 – 25 minutes. Sprinkle with cheddar and mozzarella cheese on the top and bake for approximately 5 – 10 minutes to melt the cheese. Keep this pizza aside for nearly 10 minutes before serving.

64. Vegetable Garden on Pizza

Preparation time: 10 minutes
Cooking time: 1 hour 30 minutes
Servings: 24

Ingredients:

- Pizza dough: 8 ounces
- Chopped bell pepper (green): ½ cup
- Chopped bell pepper (red): ½ cup
- Softened Cream cheese: 8 ounces
- Chopped broccoli: ½ cup
- Ranch-style dressing: 1 ounce
- Green onions (chopped): ½ cup
- Chopped carrots: 2

Directions:

1. Preheat your oven to almost 375 °F. Spread both pizza crusts on a baking pan or sheet.
2. Bake them in your preheated oven for approximately 11 – 13 minutes to make them golden brown. Keep them aside.
3. Put cream cheese in one medium bowl and mix dressing mix (1/2) in the cream cheese. You can adjust the dressing to your taste and spread this mixture over a cool crust.
4. Arrange green onions, broccoli, bell peppers, and carrots on top.
5. Chill in the fridge for almost one minute and cut into bite-size pieces to serve.

65. Alfredo Pizza with Spinach

Preparation time: 10 minutes
Cooking time: 50 minutes
Servings: 16

Ingredients:

- Chopped spinach: 10 ounces
- Mozzarella cheese (shredded): 4 cups
- Pizza crusts (raw): 2
- Alfredo sauce: 10 ounces
- Olive oil: 2 Tbsp.
- Sliced mushrooms: 6-ounce
- Artichoke hearts (quartered and drained): 10 ounces
- Black olives (sliced): 2.25 ounces
- Parmesan cheese (grated): ½ cup

Directions:

1. Preheat your oven to almost 350 °F. Spread both pizza crusts on a greased baking pan or sheet.
2. Put Alfredo sauce and spinach in one saucepan and cook over medium heat. Stir occasionally until warm.
3. Spread olive oil (1 Tbsp.) on every pizza crust and spoon half of spinach and Alfredo on every crust.
4. Spread artichoke hearts on the spinach layer and top every pizza with parmesan and mozzarella cheese. Sprinkle black olives and mushrooms on the top.
5. Bake each pizza (one by one) for almost 20 minutes in your preheated oven and wait a few minutes before making its slices.

66. BBQ Ranch Chicken Pizza

Preparation time: 15 minutes
Cooking time: 15 minutes
Servings: 3

Ingredients:

- 2 tubes (8 ounces each) of refrigerated crescent rolls
- 1/2 cup hickory smoke-flavored barbecue sauce, divided
- 1/4 cup prepared ranch salad dressing
- 3 cups cubed cooked chicken breasts
- 2 cups shredded pizza cheese blend

Directions:

1. Set oven to preheat at 375 °F.
2. Roll out the 2 crescent dough tubes and press them onto an ungreased 15 x 10 x 1-in. baking pan's bottom and up sides, press to seal perforations. Bake until lightly browned for 8-10 minutes.
3. In a small bowl, mix salad dressing and 1/4 cup barbecue sauce; layer atop the crust.
4. In a different bowl, toss together the chicken and the rest of the barbecue sauce. Layer on top.
5. Sprinkle the top with cheese.
6. Bake until cheese is melted and crust is golden brown, about another 15-20 minutes.

67. BBQ Brisket Flatbread Pizzas

Preparation time: 03 hours 00 minutes
Cooking time: 20 minutes
Servings: 3

Ingredients:

- 2 cups barbecue sauce, divided
- 1/2 cup cider vinegar
- 1/2 cup chopped green onions, divided
- 1/2 cup minced fresh cilantro, divided
- 2 pounds of fresh beef brisket
- 1 teaspoon salt
- 1 teaspoon pepper
- 1 large red onion, cut into thick slices
- 1 teaspoon olive oil
- 2 cups shredded smoked Gouda cheese

For the Dough:

- 2 ¾ to 3 ¼ cups all-purpose flour
- 1 tablespoon sugar
- 3 teaspoons salt
- 1 package (1/4 ounce) quick-rise yeast
- 1 ¼ cups warm water (120° to 130°)
- 2 tablespoons olive oil

Directions:

1. Mix a quarter cup of cilantro, a quarter cup of green onions, vinegar, and a cup of barbecue sauce in a big sealable plastic bag. Scatter pepper and salt on the brisket; put it in the bag. Enclose the bag and coat by flipping. Chill for 8 hours or up to overnight.
2. Let drain and throw away the marinade. With a drip pan, have the grill ready for indirect heat. Put brisket on top of pan; grill with cover for an hour, on low indirect heat. To coals, put 10 briquettes. Cover and let grill for an additional 1 ¼ hours or till meat is tender once pricked with a fork, putting additional briquettes if necessary. Once cool enough to hold, put meat apart using 2 forks; reserve.
3. In the meantime, mix yeast, salt, sugar, and 2 ¾ cups flour in a big bowl. Put oil and water; whisk barely till smooth. Mix in sufficient leftover flour to make a soft dough, and dough will become gooey.
4. Transfer to a floured surface area; knead for about 6 to 8 minutes till pliable and smooth. Put in an oiled bowl, flipping one time to oil the surface. Put on cover and allow to rise in a warm area till doubled in size, approximately an hour. Deflate the dough; split it in half. Roll every half into a 15-inch round.
5. Over moderate heat, grill every round with the cover on for 1 to 2 minutes per side or till slightly browned. Reserve. Brush oil on onion; grill until soft for 4 to 5 minutes, flipping once. Take off from heat; slice and reserve.
6. Scatter the rest of the barbecue sauce on the grilled side of every crust. Put the shredded brisket, onion, cheese, and the rest of the cilantro and green onions on top.
7. Put the pizza on the grill; place cover and cook on moderate indirect heat for 8 to 10 minutes or until the cheese melts and the crust is slightly browned. Through cooking, turn the pizza midway to guarantee an evenly browned crust. Redo with the rest of the pizza.

68. Feta Spinach Pizza

Preparation time: 15 minutes
Cooking time: 15 minutes
Servings: 3

Ingredients:

- 1 tube (13.8 ounces) refrigerated pizza crust
- 1 tablespoon olive oil
- 1 teaspoon minced garlic
- 1 can (15 ounces) pizza sauce
- 2 cups chopped fresh spinach
- 3/4 cup sliced red onion, separated into rings
- 1 cup sliced fresh mushrooms
- 1 cup shredded part-skim mozzarella cheese
- 1/2 cup crumbled feta cheese
- 1 teaspoon dried basil
- 1 teaspoon Italian seasoning
- Crushed red pepper flakes, optional

Directions:

1. In a greased 15 x 10 x 1-inch baking pan, unroll the crust.
2. Flatten the dough and slightly build up its edges. Then brush with oil and sprinkle garlic. Spread the pizza sauce.
3. Layer with cheese, mushrooms, onion, and spinach.
4. If desired, sprinkle with pepper flakes, Italian seasoning, and basil.
5. Bake until golden brown or for 15 to 18 minutes at 400 °F.

69. Fresh Veggie Pizza

Preparation time: 25 minutes
Cooking time: 20 minutes
Servings: 3

Ingredients:

- 1 tube (8 ounces) reduced-fat crescent rolls
- 1 package (8 ounces) of reduced-fat cream cheese
- 1 envelope ranch salad dressing mix
- 2 tablespoons fat-free milk
- 1/2 cup of each chopped fresh broccoli, cauliflower, carrots, green pepper, sweet red pepper, and mushrooms

Directions:

1. Unroll the crescent dough roll into one long rectangle. Press at the bottom of a 13x9-in. baking pan that's coated with cooking spray. Seal perforations and seams.
2. Bake for 11-13 minutes or until golden brown at 375 °F. Completely cool.
3. Beat milk, salad dressing mix, and cream cheese until smooth in a big bowl. Spread onto crust. Sprinkle with veggies.
4. Refrigerate, covered, for at least an hour prior to serving.
5. Cut to 16 pieces.

70. Fruity Brownie Pizza

Preparation time: 20 minutes
Cooking time: 15 minutes
Servings: 3

Ingredients:

- 8 ounces of cream cheese, softened
- 1/3 cup sugar
- 1 package fudge brownie mix (8-inch square pan size)
- 3/4 cup pineapple tidbits with juice
- 1 small firm banana, sliced
- 1 medium kiwifruit, peeled and sliced
- 1 cup sliced fresh strawberries
- 1/4 cup chopped pecans
- 1-ounce semisweet chocolate
- 1 tablespoon butter

Directions:

1. According to the package directions, prepare the brownie batter, then spread it on a greased 12 inches pizza pan. Bake it at 375 °F until a toothpick inserted in the middle comes out clean, about 15 to 20 minutes. Let it completely cool.
2. Beat sugar and cream cheese until smooth in a big bowl, then spread it on top of the brownie crust. Drain the pineapple, setting its juice aside. Mix the juice and banana slices together, then drain thoroughly. Over the cream cheese layer, arrange pineapple, strawberries, kiwi, and banana. Sprinkle with pecans.
3. Melt butter and chocolate in a small microwave and stir until smooth. Drizzle on top of the fruit.
4. Cover and put it in the refrigerator for an hour.

71. Seafood Pizza

Preparation time: 40 minutes
Cooking time: 20 minutes
Servings: 2
Difficulty: Low
Cost: Low

Ingredients:

For the Dough:

- 1¼ cups warm water
- 1/4 cup Extra virgin olive oil
- 1 tsp Barley malt
- 5¼ cups all-purpose flour
- 1/2 tbsp Salt
- 1 tbsp Brewer's yeast

For the Filling:

- 12 oz prawns, cooked
- 12 oz mussels, cooked
- 1 cup Tomato sauce
- 16 oz clams, cooked
- Extra virgin olive oil
- Salt to taste
- 1 sprig Parsley

Directions:

1. To make the pizza dough, mix together the salt, malt, and flour in a bowl. Dissolve the yeast in the warm water and then add the water, oil, and the yeast mixture to the bowl. Mix everything until you have a smooth dough.
2. Form the dough into a ball and place it in a bowl. Cover the bowl with plastic wrap and let it rise in a warm place for at least 4 hours or until doubled in size.
3. Divide the dough into two parts, form two loaves and let them rest on a floured surface for 1 hour at room temperature, covered with a cloth to prevent drying.
4. Roll out each loaf into a sheet the size of a baking pan and place them in greased trays.
5. Spread a layer of tomato puree over the pizzas, drizzle with oil, season with salt and bake for 8 minutes in a preheated oven at 200°F.
6. Remove the pizzas from the oven and top with the cooked prawns, mussels, and clams. Bake for another 5 minutes, making sure the seafood doesn't dry out.
7. After removing from the oven, sprinkle with chopped parsley.
8. Serve and enjoy your seafood pizza.

72. Sea and Mountains Pizza

Preparation time: 20 minutes
Cooking time: 40 minutes
Servings: 4

Ingredients:

- 2 cups all-purpose flour
- 1/4 cup olive oil
- 1 lb. bread dough
- 1 tbsp. chopped fresh parsley
- 3 cloves garlic, minced
- 5 medium-sized ripe tomatoes, sliced
- 1/4 cup white wine
- 1 lb. mussels, cleaned
- 2 tbsp. unsalted butter
- 1 tsp. salt
- 1 tsp. black pepper
- 1 lb. fresh mushrooms, sliced

Directions:

1. Clean and debeard the mussels. In a large saucepan, bring the mussels, a little water, and white wine to a boil. Cover the saucepan and cook until the mussels have opened, about 5-7 minutes. Discard any mussels that do not open.
2. In a large saucepan, heat 1/4 cup of olive oil over medium heat. Add the minced garlic and cook until fragrant, about 30 seconds. Add the sliced mushrooms and season with 1 tsp. of salt and 1 tsp. of black pepper. Cook, stirring occasionally, until the mushrooms are tender and lightly browned, about 5-6 minutes.
3. Preheat your oven to 200°F. Roll out the bread dough on a floured surface to fit a greased baking sheet. Place the sliced tomatoes on top of the bread dough. Sprinkle with a little salt and drizzle with some oil. Bake for 15 minutes.
4. Remove the baking sheet from the oven and place the mussels on top of the tomatoes. Spoon the mushroom mixture over the mussels. Return to the oven and bake for an additional 10 minutes.
5. Sprinkle with chopped parsley before serving.

73. Ham and Mushrooms Pizza

Preparation time: 10 minutes
Cooking time: 20 minutes
Servings: 4

Ingredients:

- 7.05 oz. Mushrooms in oil
- 1 1/3 cups Tomato sauce
- 4¼ cups Bread dough
- 2¼ cups Mozzarella
- Basil
- 3½ tbsp Extra virgin olive oil
- Garlic to taste
- Salt and Pepper to Taste
- 5.2 oz. Baked Ham

Directions:

1. In preparing the ham and mushroom pizza, take 1 tablespoon of extra virgin olive oil and bread dough. Roll it on a floured work surface and make a sheet of 1 cm thickness.
2. On the pizza, put the tomato puree and add the clean and well-chopped garlic.
3. Then cut the baked ham into strips and then sprinkle on the whole pizza.
4. Lastly, add the mozzarella tubes and in the oil, add the mushrooms. Season with pepper and extra virgin olive oil.
5. Put it in a hot oven to bake at 250 °F for about 15 minutes.
6. Serve the ham and mushroom pizza while hot.

74. Mexican Pizza Recipe

Preparation time: 20 minutes
Cooking time: 30 minutes
Servings: 4

Ingredients:

For the Dough:

- 1 cup warm water plus, "plus" means this ingredient in addition to the one on the next line, often with divided uses
- 2 tablespoons warm water
- 2 1/2 teaspoons active dry yeast
- 1/2 teaspoon sugar
- 3 tablespoons peanut oil
- 2 ⅓ cups all-purpose flour
- 2/3 cup cornmeal plus additional for sprinkling pizza pan
- 1 teaspoon salt
- 1/2 teaspoon ground cumin

for sauce

- 1 1/2 pound fresh tomatillos, husks discarded
- 1 small onion, sliced thin
- 2 garlic cloves, sliced thin
- 2 tablespoons peanut oil
- 1/4 cup packed fresh coriander sprigs, washed, dried, and chopped
- 1 tablespoon fresh lime juice
- 1 pound fresh chorizo, casings discarded
- 1 1/2 cup grated mexican blend cheese or cheddar
- 2 fresh poblano chilies, roasted and cut into thin strips
- 2 scallions, sliced thin
- 1/4 cup thinly sliced drained pimento-stuffed green olives
- 1/4 cup cooked black beans, rinsed if canned

Directions:

1. Make the dough in a small saucepan, heat 1/2 cup water to 110 °F.
2. Transfer to a large bowl. Stir in yeast and sugar and let stand 5 minutes, or until foamy. Stir in remaining water and dough ingredients to form a dough and on a lightly floured surface knead until smooth and elastic, about 10 minutes.
3. Put dough in a lightly oiled deep bowl, turn to coat, and let rise, covered loosely, in a warm place until doubled in bulk, about 1 hour. (alternatively, let dough rise, covered loosely, in refrigerator overnight, or until doubled in bulk.)
4. Make sauce: in a 4-quart saucepan of boiling water blanch tomatillos 1 minute and drain in a colander. Cut each tomatillo into 8 wedges. In a large heavy skillet cook onion and garlic in oil over moderate heat, stirring occasionally, until onion is pale golden. Add tomatillos and cook over moderate heat, stirring occasionally, until tomatillos are softened and mixture is reduced to about 1 1/4 cups.
5. Cool mixture slightly and in a food processor purée until smooth. Transfer sauce to a bowl and stir in coriander, lime juice, and salt to taste.

6. In a large heavy skillet cook sausage over moderately high heat, stirring and breaking up lumps, until cooked through and browned. Transfer sausage with a slotted spoon to paper towels to drain.

7. Preheat oven to 525 °F. Adjust oven rack on top shelf. Sprinkle a 16-inch perforated pizza pan with additonal cornmeal. Punch down dough and on a lightly floured work surface with a floured rolling pin roll out into a 17-inch circle.

8. Fit dough into pan, forming an edge, and bake 5 minutes. Spread sauce over partially cooked dough, leaving a 1/2-inch border around edge, and sprinkle with sausage, cheese, chilies, scallions, olives, and beans. Bake pizza 10 minutes, or until cheese is melted and crust is pale golden.

9. To roast peppers using a long-handled fork char the peppers over an open flame, turning them, for 2 to 3 minutes, or until the skins are blackened. (or broil the peppers on the rack of a broiler pan under a preheated broiler about 2 inches from the heat, turning them every 5 minutes, for 15 to 25 minutes, or until the skins are blistered and charred.)

10. Transfer the peppers to a bowl and let them steam, covered, until they are cool enough to handle. Keeping the peppers whole, peel them starting at the blossom end, cut off the tops, and discard the seeds and ribs.

75. Mexican Salmon Pizza Recipe

Preparation time: 20 minutes
Cooking time: 10 minutes
Servings: 4

Ingredients:

- Nonstick cooking spray
- 2 small purchased baked pizza crusts (about 7 inches in diameter)
- 1/2 cup bottled salsa or picante sauce
- 1/2 cup coarsely crushed tostadas
- 1/2 cup cooked, flaked salmon
- 1/4 cup chopped red onion (optional)
- 1 cup shredded mexican seasoned cheeseor monterey jack cheese

Directions:

1. A packaged combination of cheddar, Colby and monterey jack cheeses with mexican seasonings.
2. Heat oven to 450 °F.
3. Spray top surface of each pizza crust with nonstick spray and place on a baking sheet.
4. Spread half of the salsa on each crust.
5. Top each crust with crushed tostadas, salmon, onions and cheese.
6. Bake until cheese is bubbly and lightly browned, 8-10 minutes.

76. Amazing Whole Wheat Pizza Crust Recipe

Preparation time: 20 minutes
Cooking time: 20 minutes
Servings: 4

Ingredients:

- 1 teaspoon white sugar
- 1 1/2 cups warm water (110 °F/45 °C)
- 1 tablespoon active dry yeast
- 1 tablespoon olive oil
- 1 teaspoon salt
- 2 cups whole wheat flour
- 1 1/2 cups all-purpose flour

Directions:

1. In a large bowl, dissolve sugar in warm water. Sprinkle yeast over the top, and let stand for about 10 minutes, until foamy.
2. Stir the olive oil and salt into the yeast mixture, then mix in the whole wheat flour and 1 cup of the all-purpose flour until dough starts to come together. Tip dough out onto a surface floured with the remaining all-purpose flour, and knead until all of the flour has been absorbed, and the ball of dough becomes smooth, about 10 minutes.
3. Place dough in an oiled bowl, and turn to coat the surface. Cover loosely with a towel and let stand in a warm place until doubled in size, about 1 hour.
4. When the dough is doubled, tip the dough out onto a lightly floured surface, and divide into 2 pieces for 2 thin crust, or leave whole to make one thick crust. Form into a tight ball. Let rise for about 45 minutes, until doubled.
5. Preheat the oven to 425 °F (220 °C). Roll a ball of dough with a rolling pin until it will not stretch any further. Then, drape it over both of your fists, and gently pull the edges outward, while rotating the crust. When the circle has reached the desired size, place on a well oiled pizza pan. Top pizza with your favorite toppings (sauce, cheese, meats, or vegetables).
6. Bake for 16 to 20 minutes (depending on thickness) in the preheated oven, until the crust is crisp and golden at the edges, and cheese is melted on the top.

77. Basic Pizza Dough Recipe

Preparation time: 20 minutes
Cooking time: 25 minutes
Servings: 4

Ingredients:

- 2 packages dry yeast
- 1 1/2 cup lukewarm water
- 4 cups flour
- 1 teaspoon salt
- 1/2 teaspoon sugar
- 1 tablespoon olive oil

Directions:

1. Dissolve yeast in water; set aside for 5 minutes, stirring occasionally.
2. Combine flour, salt, sugar and oil in bowl; make a well in the center. When water/yeast mixture is bubbly, pour into the center of well. Start kneading dough, bringing flour toward center of bowl; gradually increase kneading motion.
3. If dough feels dry, add a little more water; if it feels sticky, add more flour. Knead vigorously until dough is smooth and elastic. Roll into ball; cover with a damp cloth. Let rest for about 20 minutes in warm place. Beat dough with your palm to expel gas formed while fermenting. Roll dough again into ball; place in greased bowl. Baste with oil. Cover with plastic wrap; store in refrigerator.
4. When ready to use, place dough on floured counter top or table. Flatten with your hands, working from center out (a rolling pin may do also). Push dough evenly onto greased cookie sheet or pizza pan, center out (a rolling pin may do also). Push dough evenly onto greased cookie sheet or pizza pan, inch circle with edges thicker than middle.
5. Apply favorite topping in desired amounts.
6. Bake in hot oven (475 to 500 °F) until golden brown.

78. Pourable Pizza Crust Recipe

Preparation time: 20 minutes
Cooking time: 35 minutes
Servings: 4

Ingredients:

- 3 tablespoons instant high active dry yeast
- Warm water (110 °F) (just enough to dissolve the active yeast)
- 7 pounds all-purpose or bread flour
- 1 package (1 lb 2 1/2 oz.) Instant nonfat dry milk
- 8 ¾ ounces sugar
- 1 1/4 teaspoon salt
- 1/8 cup olive oil

Directions:

1. Dissolve dry yeast in warm water. Let stand for 5 minutes.
2. Place flour, milk, sugar, and salt in mixer bowl. Using a whip, blend on low speed for 8 minutes. Add dissolved yeast and oil. Blend on medium speed for 10 minutes. Batter will be lumpy.
3. Oil three sheet pans (18" x 26" x 1"). Sprinkle each pan with 1 oz (approximately 3 tbsp) cornmeal. Pour or spread 3 lb 6 oz (1 1/2 quart) batter into each pan. Let stand for 25 minutes.
4. Bake until crust is set: conventional oven: 475 °F, 10 minutes.
5. Convection oven: 425 °F, 7 minutes. Top each prebaked crust with desired topping.
6. Bake until heated through and cheese is melted: conventional oven: 475 °F, 10-15 minutes.
7. Convection oven: 425 °F, 5 minutes.

79. Thin Crust Pizza Dough Recipe

Preparation time: 20 minutes
Cooking time: 30 minutes
Servings: 4

Ingredients:

- 3 cups bread flour
- 7/8 cup warm water
- 1 tablespoon vegetable shortening (crisco)
- 1 teaspoon active dry yeast
- 1 teaspoon salt
- 1/2 teaspoon sugar

Directions:

1. In a heavy-duty stand mixer fitted with dough hook, add the water, shortening, yeast, and sugar. Mix thoroughly until yeast has fully dissolved. Add flour and salt. Mix on low until most of the flour and water has mixed, then continue kneading for 10 minutes. The dough will be loose and scrappy at first and will eventually form a cohesive ball. There should be no raw flour or crumbs remaining in the bowl.
2. The dough will be somewhat dry and dense. Place the dough ball into a large bowl and cover tightly with plastic wrap. Let the dough rise for 24 hours in the refrigerator before using. Please note that I cannot over-emphasize the importance of a 24-hour rising time since it is absolutely essential so that the dough will develop its signature texture and, more importantly, its unique flavor! Do not skip this step!
3. Preheat your oven to 500 °F about one hour before you plan to bake the pizza. Turn the dough out onto a large surface and dust with flour. Using a heavy rolling pin, roll the dough out very thin to form a 24-inch or larger circle. If you're using a cutter pizza pan (recommended), dust the pan lightly with flour, place the dough in the pan and dock. Use the rolling pin to trim off the excess dough drooping over the sides of the pan. If you wish to cook the pizza directly on a pizza stone (not using a pan), then place the dough on a dusted pizza-peel, dock, and fold the edge over 1-inch all the way around and pinch it up to form a raised lip or rim.
4. Next, precook the crust for 4 minutes before adding any sauce or toppings. Remove the crust from the oven and pop any large air pockets that may have formed.
5. Add your sauce, shredded mozzarella cheese, and your favorite toppings. Continue baking, rotating the pan half way through so that it cooks evenly, until crust is sufficiently browned and crisp, about 10 to 15 minutes.
6. Remove the pizza from the oven and slide pizza out of cooking pan onto a large wire cooling rack or cutting board. Allow to cool for 5 minutes before transferring to a serving pan. This step allows the crust to stay crisp while it cools, otherwise the trapped steam will soften the crust.
7. Once cool, use a pizza cutter to slice the pie into pieces and enjoy!

80. Whole Wheat Pizza Crust Recipe

Preparation time: 20 minutes
Cooking time: 10 minutes
Servings: 4

Ingredients:

- 1 1/4 cup warm water
- 1/4 teaspoon salt -optional
- 2 tablespoons honey or sugar
- 2 cups all-purpose flour -divided
- 1 cup whole wheat flour
- 2 teaspoons active dry yeast
- 1 tablespoon cornmeal

Directions:

1. Measure carefully, placing all ingredients except cornmeal in bread machine pan in order specified by owner's manual. Program dough cycle setting; press start.
2. Remove dough from bread machine pan; let rest 2 to 3 minutes. Pat and gently stretch dough into 14rest 2 to 3 minutes. Pat and gently stretch dough into 14-inch circle.
3. Spray 14-inch pizza pan with nonstick cooking spray; sprinkle with cornmeal, if desired.
4. Press dough into pan. Follow topping and baking directions for individual recipes.
5. 1 thick 14-inch crust is 8 servings

81. Pizza Dough

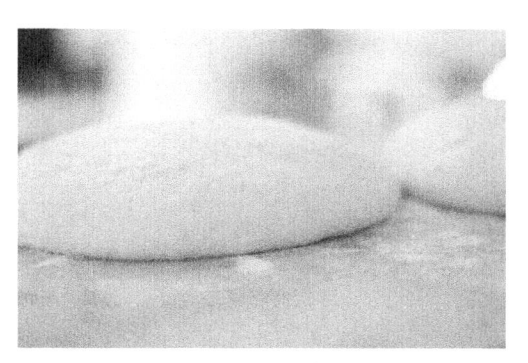

Preparation time: 20 minutes
Cooking time: 25 minutes
Servings: 12

Ingredients:

- 1 package active dry yeast
- 1 tbsp sugar
- 2 ¾ cups flour
- 2 tbsp olive oil
- 2 tbsp honey
- 2 tsp salt
- ½ tsp garlic salt

Directions:

1. In a mixing basin, combine the sugar, yeast, and a cup of warm water.
2. Allow for a 10-minute resting period.
3. Combine the remaining ingredients in a mixing bowl.
4. In a pizza pan, lay out the dough.
5. Garnish with preferred ingredients.
6. Bake at 375°F for 25 minutes.

82. Pizza with Egg-Cheese Crust

Preparation time: 20 minutes
Cooking time: 25 minutes
Servings: 12

Ingredients:

Crust:

- 4 eggs
- 6 oz. cheese (provolone or mozzarella), shredded

Toppings:

- 3 tbsp tomato sauce (unsweetened)
- 1 tsp dried oregano
- 5 oz. cheese (cheddar), grated
- 1½ oz pepperoni
- Olives (optional)

For serving:

- 2 oz. leafy greens
- 4 tbsp olive oil
- Salt, to taste
- Black pepper, to taste

Directions:

1. Set the oven temperature to 400 degrees Fahrenheit. Using parchment paper, prepare a baking sheet.
2. In a mixing dish, properly combine the eggs and cheese.
3. Place the batter on a baking pan. Form a big rectangular pizza crust with a spatula.
4. Bake for about 15 minutes or until the crust is light golden brown.
5. Bring the crust out of the oven and let it cool for a few minutes. Preheat the oven to 450°F.
6. Add oregano, tomato sauce, olives, cheese, and pepperoni to the crust.
7. Bake the crust once more until the cheese is bubbling (about 5 or 10 minutes).
8. Serve the pizza beside the salad.

83. Pro Dough

Preparation time: 20 minutes
Cooking time: 15 minutes
Servings: 12

Ingredients:

- ¼ teaspoon active dry yeast
- 1½ cups warm water
- 2 teaspoons salt
- 4 cups of all-purpose flour, more for dusting
- Extra-virgin olive oil for greasing

Directions:

1. In a medium dish, combine the yeast and warm water and let aside for 10 minutes. While the yeast is flowering, carefully clean and dry the bowl of a standing mixer. The surface should be warm to the touch. Put the flour and salt in a heated mixing basin. Mix in the yeast mixture for 2 minutes on low speed using a dough hook. The dough is ready when it is cohesive, smooth, and has pulled away from the edges of the bowl, which should take around 10 minutes of mixing at medium-low speed.
2. Return to medium-low speed and knead the dough for another 10 minutes or until it is smooth and warm to the touch.
3. Spread the dough to coat all edges of a large, lightly greased mixing bowl. Refrigerate overnight, wrapped with plastic wrap.
4. The next day, punch the dough down on a lightly floured surface. Cut it into two or four equal pieces and roll it into smooth balls. Flour the balls lightly, lay them on a baking sheet, and cover them with a moist dish towel. Let the dough rise for at least 4 hours or overnight in the refrigerator.
5. Retrieve the dough from the refrigerator and set it on a baking sheet lightly dusted with a moist kitchen towel. Allow it to rise for 1-1/2 to 2 hours or until it increases in size.
6. Continue with the chosen recipe.

84. Quick Fried Crust

Preparation time: 20 minutes
Cooking time: 5 minutes
Servings: 1

Ingredients:

- 2 eggs
- 2 tbsp parmesan cheese, grated
- 1 tbsp psyllium husk powder
- ½ tsp Italian seasoning
- Salt
- 2 tsp bacon fat (for frying)

Directions:

1. Combine the crust ingredients in a blender and blend until smooth.
2. In a pan, heat the bacon grease. Fry the crust mixture, spreading it out to make a circle.
3. When the edges of the crust begin to brown, flip it over and cook for 40-60 seconds on the other side.
4. Select your preferred toppings.

85. Roman Dough

Preparation time: 20 minutes
Cooking time: 14 minutes
Servings: 3

Ingredients:

- 2.2 lbs. Whole-wheat flour, unbleached and stoneground
- 1½ tsp Dried powdered yeast
- 1/3 cup Extra virgin olive oil
- 2¾ cups of water at room temperature
- 1½ tsp Sea salt
- ½ tsp sugar, superfine

Directions:

1. Add the flour to a mixer.
2. Dissolve the yeast in 100 mL of water, then add the flour, remaining 400 mL of water, and superfine sugar.
3. Reduce the mixer speed to low and mix for 2 minutes or until all of the water is consumed. Mix in the salt and water. Slowly, little by little, increase the mixer speed and add additional water once the preceding amount is absorbed. Don't be concerned if the mixture appears rather moist; continue mixing for 8-10 minutes, and the dough will slowly stretch and produce long gluten strands.
4. Rest the dough in a mixing basin for 10 minutes, wrapped with plastic wrap, before folding it. Allow it to develop in the refrigerator before forming it into 3 sheets of roman style pizza dough.
5. Give the dough some strength after it has rested for a few minutes. Place the dough in a work area after removing it from the container. Gently raise in the center, fold the ends, and meet in the center to generate air pockets.
6. At 90 °F, redo the fold and flip the dough. Before refolding, cover the entire bowl with clingfilm for 15 minutes.
7. Allow it to rest for another 15 minutes before folding it again. Oil a plastic jar with an airtight cover and place the dough inside. Place in the refrigerator for 18-24 hours.
8. Once the dough has matured in the refrigerator, remove it from the container, place it on a work surface, and divide it into three pieces.
9. Form each piece of dough into a ball by slipping your hands beneath the outside borders. Repeat this process multiple times until the dough forms a ball.
10. Gather and fold the edges of each piece of dough with your fingers, then bring the balls toward you. This results in a smooth and even ball. Dough balls should be allowed to rise again at room temperature for 2 hours in three oiled enclosed containers.
11. Oil a baking pan or oven tray with extra virgin olive oil. Put flour on a work surface and roll out one piece of dough. Begin by gently stretching the dough on the surface with your fingertips to fit the tray size.
12. For any pizza dough-based Roman-style pizza recipes, preheat the oven to 250 degrees Fahrenheit without using a fan.

86. Simply Amazing Pizza Dough

Preparation time: 20 minutes
Cooking time: 13 minutes
Servings: 12

Ingredients:

- 4 cups of all-purpose flour, plus for dusting
- 1½ cups warm water (about 110 °F)
- 1½ tsp salt
- 2 tbsp olive oil (extra-virgin)
- 1 package active dry yeast

Directions:

1. In a medium dish, combine the yeast with warm water and let it bloom for about 10 minutes. Add the olive oil.
2. Pulse to blend salt and flour in a food processor or standing mixer fitted with a paddle attachment. Add the yeast mixture in a slow, constant stream to the machine while running, mixing just until the dough comes together. Turn the dough out onto a well-floured board, and with lightly floured hands, knead the dough using the heels of your hands, push the dough, and then fold it over. Shape it into a ball, then cut it into 2 or 4 equal pieces.
3. Cover the dough balls with a clean dishtowel and arrange them on a lightly dusted baking sheet. For around 45 minutes, in a warm, draft-free area, you may let them rise until they've doubled in size.
4. Proceed with the desired recipe.

To Use Later:

1. Before step 3, place the dough balls on a parchment-lined baking sheet and cover them with plastic wrap.
2. Be sure to space the dough balls with room to expand, as they will double in size.
3. Refrigerate for up to 24 hours.
4. Remove from the refrigerator 15 minutes before using.

To Freeze:

1. Before step 3, dust each dough ball with flour and place it in individual resealable freezer bags. Store in the freezer for up to 1 month.
2. To use, transfer the dough to the refrigerator the night before using it.
3. The dough can also be used directly from the freezer by letting it come to room temperature for about 2 hours.

87. Skillet Pizza Crust

Preparation time: 20 minutes
Cooking time: 25 minutes
Servings: 6

Ingredients:

- 1 cup almond flour
- 3 tbsp coconut flour
- 2 tsp xanthan gum
- 1 tsp baking powder
- 25 tsp kosher salt
- 2 tsp apple cider vinegar
- 1 egg
- 5 tsp or as-needed water

Directions:

1. Finely toss the baking powder, coconut flour, xanthan gum, almond flour, and salt into a food processor. Pulse until thoroughly combined.
2. Pour in the vinegar, water, and egg (just enough for it to come together into a ball with the motor ON).
3. Wrap the dough in plastic wrap. Knead it for a minute or two. Wait for ten minutes (resting time) at room temperature or up to five days in the fridge.
4. If cooking on the stovetop, warm up the skillet using the med-high temperature while the dough rests.
5. For the oven, warm the baking pan, pizza stone, or skillet to reach 350 °F.
6. Prepare the dough between 2 sheets of baking paper (approximately 12 inches in diameter). Fold over the edges.
7. Prepare the pizza crust in the hot skillet, top-side down first, until blistered (about 2 minutes). Reduce the heat to med-low.
8. Flip the pizza crust and add the toppings of your choice. Cover with a lid.
9. When ready, serve immediately for the best results.
10. Store the dough in the refrigerator for approximately five days.

88. Spelt Pizza Dough

Preparation time: 20 minutes
Cooking time: 40 minutes
Servings: 4

Ingredients:

- 2 tsp honey
- 1 tbsp extra virgin olive oil
- 1 tsp kosher salt
- 1 package active dry yeast
- 3 cups sprouted spelt flour
- 1 cup warm water

Directions:

1. In a mixing dish, combine the water, yeast, honey, and 1 cup of flour. Allow approximately 20 minutes for the liquid to bubble and the yeast to soften.
2. Add the leftover salt, olive oil, and flour to the yeast and whisk to combine.
3. In a mixing bowl, whisk the remaining ingredients with an electric mixer fitted with a dough hook attachment and, if required, add additional flour until a tacky and soft dough is produced. This takes about 3-4 minutes.
4. Set the dough in a mixing bowl, drizzle with olive oil, and cover with a plate to rise and double in size, about 1 hour 30 minutes.
5. After pounding the dough, place it on a lightly floured work surface. Divide the mixture into four balls and cover each with plastic wrap for 30 to 45 minutes or until the dough rises slightly.
6. Finally, roll them to the thickness and form required.

89. Stuffed Crust

Preparation time: 20 minutes
Cooking time: 25 minutes
Servings: 8

Ingredients:

- 3 cups all-purpose flour
- ½ tsp salt
- 1 tbsp sugar
- 3/4 ounce (1 packet) of instant dry yeast
- 1 cup lukewarm water
- 2 tbsp olive oil
- 1/8 cup cornmeal (or all-purpose flour)
- String cheese, halved lengthwise, for stuffing or shredded mozzarella

For Sicilian Crust:

- 1/4 cup olive oil for greasing pan
- No need for cheese

Directions:

1. Whisk flour and salt together.
2. Whisk in sugar and yeast.
3. Mix in water and olive until well-moistened.
4. Knead until smooth on a floured surface (about 3-5 minutes).
5. Cover and rest the dough for 15-30 minutes.
6. Sprinkle the pizza pan with cornmeal.
7. Place dough on the center of the pan and press down with your hands to spread up the pan edge.
8. Rest the dough for 5 minutes.
9. For Sicilian Crust: Use 1/4 cup olive oil to grease a 13 x 18 inch pan. Place dough in pan and flip over. Cover with plastic wrap for 2 hours.
10. Press down along the edge again to spread so that dough hangs over the edge.
11. (Skip if Sicilian Pizza Crust) Line the edge with cheese for stuffing.
12. Fold the edge over the stuffing, pressing down to seal.
13. Top with desired sauce and toppings and bake in preheated oven at 400 °F until lightly browned (about 20-25 minutes).

90. Fruit Pizza

Preparation time: 10 minutes
Cooking time: 15 minutes
Servings: 8

Ingredients:

- 1 medium pizza base
- ½ cup strawberries, hulled and finely chopped
- ½ cup pineapple, finely chopped
- ½ cup apple, finely chopped
- 1 cup sour cream

Directions:

1. Preheat the oven to 350ºF.
2. Combine all the ingredients in a bowl except the pizza.
3. Spread the prepared mix over the pizza base.
4. Now, place the pizza over the oven's grill.
5. Bake for 10 minutes.
6. When the pizza is ready, take it out of the oven.
7. Then, transfer the pizza to a serving platter and make 6 equal slices with the help of a pizza cutter.
8. Serve hot!

91. Parsley Pizza

Preparation time: 10 minutes
Cooking time: 15 minutes
Servings: 8

Ingredients:

- 1 medium pizza base
- 2 cups mozzarella cheese, grated
- 2 cups fresh parsley leaves, finely chopped
- 2 tbsp. pizza sauce
- Dried oregano and chili flakes for seasoning
- Salt and pepper to taste

Directions:

1. Preheat the oven to 350ºF.
2. Spread a pizza sauce over the pizza base and sprinkle mozzarella over each half. Add parsley to the pizza in an even layer. Add salt and pepper.
3. Now, place the pizza over the oven's grill.
4. Bake for 15 minutes or until cheese melts completely and turns golden brown.
5. When the pizza looks ready, take it out of the oven.
6. Season with dried oregano and chili flakes.
7. Then, transfer the pizza to a serving platter and make 6 equal slices with the help of a pizza cutter,
8. Serve hot!

92. Cauliflower and Green Pea Pizza

Preparation time: 10 minutes
Cooking time: 15 minutes
Servings: 8

Ingredients:

- 1 medium pizza base
- 2 cups mozzarella cheese, grated
- 1 small head of cauliflower, grated
- 1 cup boiled green peas
- 2 tbsp. pizza sauce
- Dried oregano and chili flakes for seasoning
- Salt and pepper to taste

Directions:

1. Preheat the oven to 350 ºF.
2. Spread a pizza sauce over the pizza base and sprinkle mozzarella over each half. Add veggies to the pizza in an even layer. Add salt and pepper.
3. Now, place the pizza over the oven's grill.
4. Bake for 15 minutes or until cheese melts completely and turns golden brown.
5. Take the pizza out of the oven after it's done.
6. Season with dried oregano and chili flakes.
7. Then, transfer the pizza to a serving platter and make 6 equal slices with the help of a pizza cutter.
8. Serve hot!

93. Ricotta Cheese and Lemon Grass Pizza

Preparation time: 10 minutes
Cooking time: 15 minutes
Servings: 8

Ingredients:

- 1 medium pizza base
- 2 cups mozzarella cheese, grated
- 2 cups ricotta cheese, crumbled
- 2 tbsp. freshly chopped lemon grass
- 2 tbsp. pizza sauce
- Dried oregano and chili flakes for seasoning
- Salt and pepper to taste

Directions:

1. Preheat the oven to 350 ºF.
2. Spread a pizza sauce over the pizza base and sprinkle mozzarella over each half. Add ricotta cheese and lemon grass to the pizza in an even layer. Add salt and pepper.
3. Now, place the pizza over the oven's grill.
4. Bake for 15 minutes or until cheese melts completely and turns golden brown.
5. Take the pizza out of the oven after it's done.
6. Season with dried oregano and chili flakes.
7. Then, transfer the pizza to a serving platter and make 6 equal slices with the help of a pizza cutter.
8. Serve hot!

94. Chicken and Pineapple Pizza

Preparation time: 10 minutes
Cooking time: 15 minutes
Servings: 8

Ingredients:

- 1 medium pizza base
- 2 cups mozzarella cheese, grated
- ½ pound roasted chicken, shredded
- 1 cup pineapple, finely chopped
- 2 tbsp. pizza sauce
- Dried oregano and chili flakes for seasoning
- Salt and pepper to taste

Directions:

1. Preheat the oven to 350 ºF.
2. Spread a pizza sauce over the pizza base and sprinkle mozzarella over each half. Add chicken and pineapple to the pizza in an even layer. Add salt and pepper.
3. Now, place the pizza over the oven's grill.
4. Bake for 15 minutes or until cheese melts completely and turns golden brown.
5. Pull the pizza out of oven once it is ready.
6. Season with dried oregano and chili flakes.
7. Then, transfer the pizza to a serving platter and make 6 equal slices with the help of a pizza cutter.
8. Serve hot!

95. Salami Pizza

Preparation time: 10 minutes
Cooking time: 15 minutes
Servings: 8

Ingredients:

- 1 medium pizza base
- 2 cups mozzarella cheese, grated
- ¼ pound chicken salami, chopped
- 2 tbsp. pizza sauce
- Dried oregano and chilli flakes for seasoning
- Salt and pepper to taste

Directions:

1. Preheat the oven to 350 ºF.
2. Spread a pizza sauce over the pizza base and sprinkle mozzarella over each half. Add chopped salami to the pizza in an even layer. Add salt and pepper.
3. Now, place the pizza over the oven's grill.
4. Bake for 15 minutes or until cheese melts completely and turns golden brown.
5. Pull the pizza out of oven once it is ready.
6. Season with dried oregano and chili flakes.
7. Then, transfer the pizza to a serving platter and make 6 equal slices with the help of a pizza cutter.
8. Serve hot!

96. Pork Sausage Pizza

Preparation time: 10 minutes
Cooking time: 15 minutes
Servings: 8

Ingredients:

- 1 medium pizza base
- 2 cups mozzarella cheese, grated
- 2 cups pork sausage, chopped
- 1 large white onion, finely chopped
- 2 tbsp. pizza sauce
- Dried oregano and chilli flakes for seasoning
- Salt and pepper to taste

Directions:

1. Preheat the oven to 350 ºF.
2. Spread a pizza sauce over the pizza base and sprinkle mozzarella over each half. Add pork sausage and white onion to the pizza in an even layer. Add salt and pepper.
3. Now, place the pizza over the oven's grill.
4. Bake for 15 minutes or until cheese melts completely and turns golden brown.
5. Pull the pizza out of oven once it is ready.
6. Season with dried oregano and chili flakes.
7. Then, transfer the pizza to a serving platter and make 6 equal slices with the help of a pizza cutter.
8. Serve hot!

97. Turkey and Carrot Pizza

Preparation time: 10 minutes
Cooking time: 15 minutes
Servings: 8

Ingredients:

- 1 medium pizza base
- 2 cups mozzarella cheese, grated
- 2 cups roasted turkey, shredded
- 2 cups carrot, grated
- 2 tbsp. pizza sauce
- Dried oregano and chili flakes for seasoning
- Salt and pepper to taste

Directions:

1. Preheat the oven to 350 ºF.
2. Spread a pizza sauce over the pizza base and sprinkle mozzarella over each half. Add turkey and carrots to the pizza in an even layer. Add salt and pepper.
3. Now, place the pizza over the oven's grill.
4. Bake for 15 minutes or until cheese melts completely and turns golden brown.
5. Pull the pizza out from oven once it is ready.
6. Season with dried oregano and chili flakes.
7. Then, transfer the pizza to a serving platter and make 6 equal slices with the help of a pizza cutter.
8. Serve hot!

98. White Button Mushroom and Black Olive Pizza

Preparation time: 10 minutes
Cooking time: 15 minutes
Servings: 4

Ingredients:

- 1 medium pizza base
- 2 cups mozzarella cheese, grated
- 2 cups white button mushrooms, chopped
- 1 cup black olives, sliced
- 2 tbsp. pizza sauce
- Dried oregano and chili flakes for seasoning
- Salt and pepper to taste

Directions:

1. Preheat the oven to 350 ºF.
2. Spread a pizza sauce over the pizza base and sprinkle mozzarella over each half. Add veggies to the pizza in an even layer. Add salt and pepper.
3. Now, place the pizza over the oven's grill.
4. Bake for 15 minutes or until cheese melts completely and turns golden brown.
5. Pull the pizza out of oven once it is ready.
6. Season with dried oregano and chili flakes.
7. Then, transfer the pizza to a serving platter and make 6 equal slices with the help of a pizza cutter.
8. Serve hot!

99. Fast Pizza with Pepper, Zucchini, and Red Onion

Preparation time: 1 hour
Cooking time: 10 minutes
Servings: 4

Ingredients:

For the Dough:

- 1 cup all-purpose flour
- ½ cup butter, chilled
- 1 whole egg
- 1 pinch salt

For the Toppings:

- 1 zucchini, chopped
- 1 red onion, sliced
- 1 cup swiss cheese
- ½ red bell pepper
- ½ yellow bell pepper
- ½ green bell pepper
- 2 teaspoons tomato sauce
- ½ teaspoon balsamic vinegar
- 1 pinch of ground black pepper
- 1 pinch salt
- 1 tablespoon olive oil

Directions:

1. Preheat the oven.
2. After removing the stem and seeds, chop the peppers in the same way as the zucchini.
3. Cover the baking sheet with parchment paper and place the zucchini, onion, and peppers on it. Sprinkle with olive oil, salt, and pepper. Put the pan in the oven for 5-7 minutes.
4. To prepare the dough, pour the flour and pre-chilled butter, and salt. Crumb with a knife. Add the egg and 1 tbsp. of ice water and knead it all with your hands.
5. Roll the dough into a thin cake, place it on the baking sheet, and spread the tomato paste over it.
6. Grate the cheese on a large grater.
7. Put the cooked vegetables on the cake, sprinkle with balsamic vinegar, sprinkle with grated cheese, and place in the oven for 5-7 minutes.

100. Pizza Margherita

Preparation time: 2 hours
Cooking time: 25 minutes
Servings: 4

Ingredients:

For the Dough:

- 1 ¾ cups bread flour
- 1 ¼ cups water
- 1 tablespoon yeast
- 1 tablespoon sugar
- 1 tablespoon olive oil
- 1 tablespoon of sea salt

For the Toppings:

- 2 cups canned tomatoes
- 2 garlic cloves
- 2 tablespoons basil
- 2 tablespoons tomato paste
- 1 cup mozzarella cheese
- 2 tablespoons parmesan cheese, grated
- 2 tablespoons ground black pepper, to taste
- 2 tablespoons salt, to taste
- 1 tablespoon olive oil

Directions:

1. Mix yeast and sugar in a bowl. Add 4 tablespoons of water. Let stand in a warm place for 15 minutes until the mixture is frothed.
2. Mix the flour and the salt. Add the oil to the yeast mixture as well as the remaining water. Mix the dough with a wooden spoon.
3. Place the dough on a table sprinkled with flour, and knead for 5 minutes.
4. Return the dough to a bowl, cover it with a towel, and leave for 30 minutes or until it has risen 2 times.
5. Knead the dough for 2 more minutes; stretch it out with your hands.
6. Put the dough on a baking sheet.
7. Spread the tomato paste on the dough.
8. Put the tomatoes, garlic, basil, olive oil, salt, and pepper in a large frying pan. Cook for 20 minutes until the sauce starts to thicken. Add the tomato paste and allow it to cool slightly.
9. Cover the base with the filling, and sprinkle with mozzarella and parmesan cheese.
10. Bake pizza in a 400 °F oven for 25 minutes.
11. Remove the pizza from the oven, put it on a dish, cut it into small pieces, and serve.

101. Mixed Veggie Pizza

Preparation time: 25 minutes
Cooking time: 15 minutes
Servings: 10

Ingredients:

- 2 packages of crescent dinner rolls
- 15 ounces of cream cheese, softened
- 1 cup sour cream
- 1½ ounces dry ranch dressing mix
- 2 cups cheddar cheese
- 1 tomato, sliced
- 1 cup celery
- ½ cup green onions
- 1 cup carrots
- ½ cup green bell peppers

Directions:

1. Preheat oven to 370 °F.
2. On a flat cookie sheet, spread out the dinner rolls to make a circular shape.
3. Cook for 10 minutes in the oven until slightly golden brown.
4. Take it out and let it cool.
5. Mix cream cheese, ranch dressing mix, and sour cream in a separate bowl.
6. Spread this prepared mixture on top of the dinner rolls.
7. Chop all the vegetables according to liking.
8. Layer the chopped veggies on top of the rolls.
9. In the end, sprinkle the cheese on top. Place back in the oven until the cheese melts.
10. Cut the pizza into slices. Serve and enjoy.

102. Delightful Veggie Pizza

Preparation time: 20 minutes
Cooking time: 10 minutes
Servings: 6

Ingredients:

- 2 packages of crescent dinner rolls
- 2 cups cream cheese, softened
- 1/3 cup cucumber slices
- 1 plum tomato, seeded and chopped
- 1/6 teaspoon garlic powder
- 1 cup sour cream
- 1 teaspoon dill weed, dried
- 1 cup fresh broccoli florets
- 1 jalapeno, chopped (optional)

Directions:

1. First, preheat the oven to 375 °F.
2. Take out the dough and separate it, then cut it into 4 rectangles.
3. In a large pan, place the dough and press it to form a crust.
4. Bake in preheated oven for 10 minutes.
5. Next, let it cool.
6. Add cream cheese, dill, sour cream, and garlic powder in a small bowl.
7. Spread the mixture over the crust evenly.
8. Top with chopped vegetables.
9. Serve and enjoy.

103. Broccoli Pizza

Preparation time: 30 minutes
Cooking time: 20 minutes
Servings: 4

Ingredients:

- 2 cups all-purpose flour
- 1/3 cup milk
- 2 tablespoons olive oil
- 2 teaspoons yeast
- 1 bell pepper
- 2 cups mashed potatoes
- 2 tablespoons butter
- 1 whole egg
- 1 ½ cups broccoli
- 1 cup champignon mushrooms, sliced

Directions:

1. Mix the mashed potatoes with flour. Then add yeast diluted in warm milk, egg, melted butter, cheese, salt, and pepper, and knead the dough.
2. Put in a warm place for 2 hours.
3. Cut off the heads of the broccoli; cut the pepper into strips.
4. Put the broccoli in the microwave at full power for 3 minutes. Stir gently and then put back in for another 3 minutes.
5. Sauté the peppers and mushrooms in olive oil separately.
6. Put the dough in a greased form and sprinkle it with olive oil. Distribute evenly throughout the form.
7. Put the fillings on top - broccoli, mushrooms with pepper, and chopped mozzarella. Sprinkle with oregano.
8. Bake until ready at 400 °F for approximately 20 minutes.
9. Serve chilled.

104. Pizza Roll

Preparation time: 30 minutes
Cooking time: 40 minutes
Servings: 4

Ingredients:

- 2 cups 00 flour
- 1¼ tsp Dry brewer's yeast
- 2/3 cup Water at room temperature
- 1 tsp Salt
- 1 tsp Malt
- 1 tbsp Extra virgin olive oil

For the stuffing:

- 5 oz. Tomato sauce
- 3.5 oz. Cooked ham thinly sliced
- 5 oz. Mozzarella
- 0.35 oz. Basil

To brush

- 1 tbsp Extra virgin olive oil

Directions:

1. In making the stuffed pizza roll, begin by making the basic dough. Into a bowl, pour in the water at room temperature, add salt and use a spoon to mix in order to dissolve it. Pour in extra virgin olive oil and mix the emulsion again.
2. Sift the flour in another large bowl, then add half the water mixture, salt, oil, dehydrated beer yeast, and malt. Begin using your hands to knead, or you can also use a fork. Keep the remaining emulsion and little flour close to you which you will gradually integrate with the dough to get the consistency you desire, which must be elastic and soft based on the flour you have used; it may take less or a little more water.
3. On a surface, keep kneading until you get a soft, smooth, but consistent dough that you will use to form a ball. Leave it in the bowl and use plastic wrap to cover it. Leave it in the oven with lights on but when it is turned off, let the dough rise and double in size and volume. You will need a temperature between 26-30 °C and about 2-3 hours.
4. Meanwhile, prepare the filling ingredients. Into a bowl, pour in the tomato sauce and use basil leaves chopped with your hands, extra virgin olive oil, and salt to season.
5. Cut the mozzarella into cubes and put it in a colander to drain. It's crucial to dry

to avoid losing liquids by moistening the dough during cooking.
6. Take the dough that has doubled in volume once the leavening period is over, and take it on a lightly floured pastry board. Use a rolling pin to roll out until you get a sheet that is oval-shaped, measuring 38 x 34 cm.
7. On the pastry, sprinkle the tomato sauce and make sure to leave some centimeters from the edge. Cover the fresh basil leaves with diced mozzarella, and lastly, lay the cooked ham slices.
8. Use oil to brush the edges left to make the roll adhere well when closed. Inwardly close the edges, so they fall on the filling part and prevent the filling from coming out during the cooking.
9. Roll the dough from the longest side at this point and transfer the roll onto the dripping pan lined with parchment paper and seal the ends.
10. Use olive oil to brush the surface and bake for 40 minutes in a preheated static oven at 180 °F.
11. Remove your stuffed pizza roll from the oven and allow it to rest for at least 10 minutes before cutting it into 27 slices.

Storage

1. Your stuffed pizza roll can be stored in a refrigerator for 1 day and then heat it when you serve it.
If you have used all the fresh ingredients, you can alternatively cook it halfway and then freeze it in order to finish the cooking in the oven as required.

Tips:

The dough may be made a day ahead of time and stored in the fridge. A day at room temperature before distributing is all that is required. Try stuffing your pizza roll with grilled vegetables or different cold cuts.

105. Fried Pizza with Mortadella and Fiordilatte

Preparation time: 40 minutes
Cooking time: 5 minutes
Servings: 4

Ingredients:

- 0.1 oz Fresh brewer's yeast
- 3¼ cups 00 flour
- 1 cup Water
- 3 tsp Salt

For the Stuffing:

- ¼ cup Water
- 4.23 oz. Mortadella thick slices
- 7.76 oz. Fiordilatte mozzarella
- Black pepper to taste
- 1½ cups Buffalo ricotta
- Basil to taste

For frying:

- Peanut oil

Directions:

1. To make the fried pizza with mortadella and fiordilatte mozzarella, put the required amount of water in a large bowl, add the brewer's yeast and use your hands to dissolve it.
2. In a bowl, sift the flour, add the salt and use the back of a wooden spoon to mix. Add almost half the flour and use a spoon to stir until you obtain a batter. Carry out all these operations to respect the flour's absorption times.
3. At intervals, add the remaining flour; you will better be able to regulate the amount you add, and the dough will become softer. After using a wooden spoon to incorporate all the flour that is necessary, start using your hands to knead inside the bowl by collecting the flour on the inside edges of the bowl and bringing the dough inwards.
4. Transfer the dough to a work surface when the container is clean. It will already have its compactness though it will still be raw. Add a flour veil and for 2-3 minutes, make the folds by adding more flour. The dough shouldn't be too smooth.
5. Keep working by closing the dough in this way. Beat it on the surface by grabbing the dough in halves and creating a crease and by carrying it forward and spreading it, and it closes on itself. In such a way, the glutinic mesh will start forming, and some air will be incorporated inside. This should be done for at least 10 minutes to prevent the dough from stringing.
6. Leave the dough on the surface covered with plastic wrap and compact the loaf. After waiting for 10-15 minutes, you will notice that the dough has become silky, more compact, and smoother. This is also known as an episode. Put a little flour after removing the central notch and create a loaf.
7. Get 4 portions, and without lightning too much, pirate every portion but seal the vortex created at the bottom as well. You will get 4 spherical balls. You can

now transfer them to a food box and space them at least by 2 cm.
8. Use a lid to cover and leave them in a cool place to rise for 6-8 hours. Keep checking the leavening from time to time.
9. At this point, work on the filling ingredients. Cut the mozzarella roughly and also cut the fiordilatte mozzarella in slices, then in small pieces. Transfer the ricotta to a bowl; add some water and then work on it until you get a creamy and smooth, consistent dough. Put the oil to heat once the dough has risen and it will reach 200 °F temperature.
10. Use a well-floured stick and take the dough ball by detaching it from the bottom. Use dry hands to spread it after putting it on the surface. You will need to get a smaller disk than the usual pizza. In the center, put ¼ of the ricotta, leaving 3 cm from the edge clean.
11. Add some mortadella of black pepper that has been grated at the moment, fiordilatte mozzarella, and basil leaves.
12. Then close the crescent pizza using your fingers by squeezing to seal the edges well. Use your fists to squeeze the edge again and ensure no holes. Lift and transfer it to a pan with boiling oil, and it will stretch naturally, then dip it in hot oil.
13. You can use two skimmers. Keep the pizza immersed using one and move the oil over it using the other. Turn it upside down and keep cooking until it's golden brown after waiting for a few minutes.
14. Put it on a tray with fried paper after draining it and continue with preparing and cooking others. Serve and enjoy your hot fried pizzas.

106. Pear and Brie Pizza

Preparation time: 45 minutes
Cooking time: 25 minutes
Servings: 4

Ingredients:

- 1½ cups Water
- 1/4 cup Extra virgin olive oil
- 4 1/2 cups Flour 0
- 2 teaspoons Salt
- 1 packet Dry yeast

For the Dressing:

- 1/4 cup Grated Parmesan Cheese
- 2/3 cup Brie cheese
- 3 medium Williams pears
- 2 cups Mozzarella cheese

Directions:

1. Place the flour in a mixing bowl and make a well in the center. Add 1/2 cup of water and the yeast and mix until well combined.
2. Gradually add the remaining water and continue mixing until you have a smooth dough.
3. Gradually add the oil and continue mixing until the oil is fully incorporated.
4. Remove the dough from the mixing bowl and shape it into a ball. Place the dough in a lightly oiled bowl, cover with a clean towel, and let it rise in a warm place until doubled in size, about 1 hour.
5. Preheat oven to 400°F (200°C).
6. Divide the dough into 4 equal parts and shape each into a ball. Cover with a clean towel and let rest for 30 minutes.
7. Roll out each ball of dough into a round shape. Place the dough rounds on a lightly greased pizza pan or baking sheet.
8. Sprinkle the mozzarella cheese evenly over the dough rounds. Cut the brie into small squares and arrange over the mozzarella.
9. Chop and peel the pears, then slice into equal-thickness pieces and remove the core. Arrange the pear slices on the pizzas in a radial design.
10. Sprinkle the grated Parmesan cheese over the pizzas. Bake for 10-15 minutes, or until the crust is golden brown and the cheese is melted.
11. Serve hot. Enjoy!

CHAPTER 6: FAQs

How to Cook Pizza in the Home Oven?

To cook pizza in a home oven, start by preparing the dough. Preheat your oven to the desired temperature, typically around 425-450°F. Place the pizza on a baking sheet or pizza stone and bake for 8-12 minutes or until the crust is golden brown and the cheese is melted.

It's important to consider the type of oven you have and the thickness of your pizza crust when determining the cooking time. You may need to adjust the temperature or cooking time based on your oven and preferences. Experimenting with different techniques, such as using a pizza stone or using a higher temperature for a shorter time, can help you find the method that works best for you.

Temperature of Cooking:

When using a wooden oven, the best temperature range for making a good pizza is 380-450 °F. Temperatures not exceeding 250 °F are recommended for the gas oven. It functions similarly to the wooden oven.

The ideal temperature for cooking pizza depends on the type of oven and the type of pizza you are making. In general, the recommended temperature range for cooking pizza in a wood-fired oven is around 700-800°F. This high heat creates a crispy crust and perfectly melted cheese.

For a gas oven, the recommended temperature is 350-400°F. This temperature range creates a crispy crust and well-cooked toppings, while also mimicking the high heat of a wood-fired oven. However, the exact temperature will vary depending on the specific gas oven and the type of pizza being made. It may be helpful to experiment with different temperatures and cooking times to find the best results for your specific oven and preferences.

Homemade Pizza Cooking Time:

The cooking time for a homemade pizza varies depending on the type of oven used and the desired level of doneness.

In a professional gas or electric oven, a pizza typically takes around 6-8 minutes to cook at 450-500°F. However, the exact cooking time will depend on the thickness of the dough, the toppings used, and the desired level of doneness.

In a standard home oven, a pizza typically takes around 12-15 minutes to cook at 450°F. However, the exact cooking time will depend on the oven's temperature accuracy and the desired level of doneness.

In a wood-fired oven, the cooking time will depend on the oven's temperature and the desired level of doneness. A wood-fired oven typically takes around 30 minutes to reach a temperature of 700-800°F. Once the oven is preheated, a pizza can be cooked in as little as 90 seconds to 2 minutes.

Cooking a pizza on a plate using a wood oven can be challenging and is not recommended for inexperienced cooks. It is important to continuously turn the pizza to prevent burning, and the cooking time will depend on the oven's temperature and the desired level of doneness.

Are you using the right yeast?

The yeast used in making pizza dough is an important factor in the end result. Many expert pizza makers use "mother yeast," which is a type of natural yeast, while others use commercially available active dry yeast. Using less yeast will result in a longer rising time, and some pizza makers prefer to let the dough rise in a refrigerator for a slow, cool fermentation process.

Choosing the Flour: Is one worth the other?

Absolutely not. Quality flour brings forth quality pizza. Flour 0 is highly recommended by pizza chefs. It is recommended to use a mixture with Manitoba flour if the dough is very soft. It would help to buy the flour from the mill to get a high-quality dough.

Should the salt be added? If yes, when?

Yes, the salt can be added, but at the end. This is because the salt sterilizes the yeast's action as a disinfectant.

Do I need to add sugar?

Yes, it is a very important ingredient that stimulates leavening and should be added to the yeast. You can alternatively use malt or honey.

Rolling Pin; should I use it?

Using a rolling pin to flatten your homemade pizza dough is a recommended technique, especially if you don't feel confident in using your hands. Some finesse is required in this process.

What is the reason behind the so much melting of mozzarella in homemade pizza?

Regarding the excessive melting of mozzarella on homemade pizza, this is often due to the high whey content in traditional mozzarella cheese. To avoid this, try slicing the cheese and draining it in a colander for 2-3 hours before adding it to the pizza.

Is it right to fill the pizza with other ingredients before you bake it?

No, it is wrong. If you fill the ingredients before baking, they will burn even before baking. It is ideal baking the pizza with tomato only, and when about to end cooking, add mozzarella and then the ingredients. Ham should come in at the end.

What is the ideal temperature?

The ideal temperature for cooking pizza in a domestic oven can vary, but a temperature of 425-450 °F is commonly recommended. The specific temperature and placement of the pizza in the oven will depend on the specific oven and the desired outcome. It is best to consult the oven's manual. It is generally not recommended to cook pizza at a temperature higher than the maximum temperature recommended by the oven manufacturer.

CONCLUSION

Thank you for reading this book. There is no other dish more popular in the United States than a pizza. Pizza is the ideal dish for any picky eater in your household. Pizza is one of the world's most basic and popular dishes, but it is also most difficult to describe. Pizza preparation is simple, with few rules that determine a sublime product. The dough is made with only flour, natural yeast, salt, and water. The dough is then hand-kneaded or combined before being punched and formed by hand.

You now understand the fundamental components of each homemade pizza, how to make them, and how to assemble your own culinary masterpiece. You can now have your pizza and eat it as well at a much lower cost than ordering out...all from the comfort of your own home.

But, because knowledge is only half the battle, what you learned in this book is only half the pizza. To complete the picture, you must put them to the test. Begin by preparing the dough, one of the sauce recipes, and three toppings. If your first experiment goes differently than planned, note what you think went wrong and try again. Try and try again until you get it right.

The next step is for you to start making all of the pizza recipes you've discovered in this book. After you've completed that, it's time to try your hand at making your own pizza dishes from scratch.

We've laid the groundwork for you to become a pizza connoisseur in this cookbook. You'll be an expert in the bases, sauces, and toppings, and you'll be able to make amazing pizzas at home.

These recipes are sure to please everyone in your life. Adults, children, healthy eaters, and junk food lovers will all be satisfied, and the cook will receive all the credit.

The recipes were designed to be shared. This is an activity book for family and friends, not just a cookbook.

Good luck!

ALPHABETICAL INGREDIENTS INDEX

B

Bacon And Spinach Pizza, 57

Basil garlic sauce, 88

BBQ Brisket Flatbread Pizzas, 109

BLT Pizza, 55

Buttermilk Biscuit Dough, 104

Butternut Squash Pizzas with Rosemary, 30

C

Cajun Shrimp and Scallop Pizza, 31

Caramel Apple Pizza, 33

Caramelized Onion and Ricotta Cheese Pizza, 34

Cauliflower pizza, 67

Cauliflower-Spinach Pizza, 39

Cheese and Almond Pizza, 43

Cheeseburger Pizza, 45

Colorful Crab Appetizer Pizza, 58

D

Dartboard Pizza, 61

F

Four-cheese pizza, 73

Fresh vegetable pizza, 100

M

Mexican pita pizzas (mexico) recipe, 65

Mayonnaise burrito pizzas recipe, 51

N

New York Style Pizza, 29

P

Pan Pizza Crust, 82

Pizza napolitano, 91

S

Satay Pizza with Chicken, 49

T

Tuna pizza, 77

V

Vegetable Garden on Pizza, 106

Y

Yeast-free pizza dough, 86

Made in the USA
Monee, IL
20 February 2023